NATION-BUILDING

How to Build *and* Sustain *a*
Developed Nigeria

By Bobby Udoh

Published in Nigeria in 2011

Cover design/text layout: Jon Whitty (worldofjon@hotmail.com)

ISBN 1463766882

Dedication

To my children
Esther and Stephen
You are nation-builders

To every Nigerian
Investing their time, money and talent to
Build a great Nigeria

Contents

Acknowledgements

I thank my God and Father of our Lord Jesus for sowing this book in my spirit after I sought him in prayers to change Nigeria. I acknowledge the grace He gave me to seek solutions rather than focus on problems and to keep the thoughts in this book simple. I thank Him for the passion to start and the willpower to complete this book.

God works through people and the first person I would like to acknowledge is the senior pastor of our church, Kensington Temple, Colin Dye. Your teaching, inspiration and lifestyle gave me the courage to undertake the writing of this book. You believe and have made us believe that as children of God we have to become agents of change in our nation, making it a society of justice, equality of people of all faith and background and social equity. This book and more importantly the mission to build a developed Nigeria came from your inspiration. I thank you for nursing this book to fruition

I am also grateful for the support of my cell leader, Dudley Hanciles. You helped nurture this vision and was there every step of the way. Your continuous support strengthens our belief that whatever challenges we face in our effort to build a developed Nigeria can and will be conquered.

To all my friends who encouraged me to publish this book because of their faith in Nigeria and in my vision, I say thank you. I acknowledge Imoh Udom, Franklin Nwankwo, Dele Olawoye, Tunde Isaac, Bassey Antiah, Edet Umoren, Ekaete Enodien, Bobby Edet, IB Udofia, Paddy Anigbo and Kieron Osmotherly. I am particularly grateful to two of my friends, my in-law, John Soberekon who stood by me from start to finish, encouraging in words and in deeds, your faith in this vision helped to be keep the fire burning; and my friend who is closer than a brother, Iso Bassey, who played a primary role in moving me from a place of thought to a place of action and participating in every stage of the process. With friends such as this, our dream of a developed Nigeria will come to pass.

What a blessing to finally find you my twin brother, Fela Durotoye. We are not biological twins but we are twins in vision and purpose. God has brought us together to fulfil all He has in store for us to accomplish. I thank you for accepting to write the Foreword to this book, Nigeria is blessed to have you, whom I call an apostle (a forerunner), together we shall raise nation-builders who will build Nigeria into the most desirable country by 2025.

My late father, O. W. Udoh, a renowned journalist and PR expert, your love for writing made an impact on me and your offer to proofread my book encouraged me. This is an effort to see your dream of a developed Nigeria become a reality. You believed in this country despite the injustice you suffered and this has enabled me believe in Nigeria irrespective of the circumstances. I acknowledge you the great Nigerian.

I thank my loving step-mother, Nora Udoh, who is ever ready to encourage and challenge me to step out in faith. My elder brother, Willy Udoh, I acknowledge you and I know when your book gets published it will be a blessing to many in our nation. To my other siblings, Favour, Inyang, Mfon, Ofonime, Uduak, Eno, Bassey, Nyakno, and my uncles, aunties and in-laws, I am grateful for your encouragement and support.

I thank my wife, Bubu, for accommodating the craziness and the sacrifice involved in pursuing a vision, especially when the vision involves developing Nigeria. I pray that you will see the rise of nation-builders and a developed Nigeria in your lifetime. I also acknowledge my children Esther and Stephen. I desire strongly that in your lifetime you will live in a developed Nigeria and you will give yourself to the sustenance of that development. I love you three very much.

The project was finished in the hands of my copy-editor

Adekemi Kudehinbu and my graphic designer Jon Whitty. I can not thank you enough for making me a novice feel like an expert. I stretched your patience, tested your expertise and pushed boundaries, in the end we came up with something unique. Thank you Adekemi for your enormous contribution to this work. To Jon, I also say thank you for giving yourself, not just your work. You had the last sign off and so I sign off my acknowledgements with you two. God bless you.

Foreword

I have always believed that a nation is not the bridges, roads or the vegetation in its geographical space. Rather, a nation is defined by the people in it.

To become the world's most desirable nation to live in, Nigeria must therefore first build her people. If we successfully build the people, the people will build the nation.

No wonder in May 2005, God asked me to go and raise him a Generation that is Empowered, Motivated and Stirred To Operate with Natural Excellence – G.E.M.S.T.O.N.E. These people He said, will build the nation.

Interestingly too, a people that do not share common values cannot forge a common course. That's why we have continued to proliferate the ten ideals of a true Nigerian. These ideals are products of a nation-builder's core values. They have been endorsed by about 400 leaders from the six geo-political zones in Nigeria and they will soon be signed by millions of Nigerians around the country when the 'Values scroll' begins its nationwide tour.

The ideals are to:

1. Make a positive impact on everyone you meet and every where you go.
2. Be a solution to problems and not a problem to solution.
3. Be a role model worthy of emulation.
4. Be the best at all you do, particularly what you are naturally good at.
5. Do the right thing at all times regardless of who is doing the wrong thing.
6. Value time and make the best of it.
7. Care and show respect through your words and actions.

8. Consciously build a great legacy starting today and every day.
9. Live a life of integrity and
10. Make your family, your nation and your God proud.

I would say we are blessed to have been born at such a time as this. We are the third generation of Nigerians since independence. The first was the generation of liberation; the second was that of revelation that showed forth the great potentials of Nigeria.

But we are the generation of transformation. It is our generation that has been given the awesome responsibility of transforming Nigeria's potential into reality. But the realisation of that transformation requires that each one of us begins to first and foremost, transform our own potentials into reality.

In this book, Nation-building evangelist, Bobby Udoh shows us that it is critical for every Nigerian to first become the change we desire in our nation. He notes that as long as Nigerians remain self focused, instead of looking to serve the nation, change will continue to elude us. And sadly so, because the greatness (or otherwise) of our nation is largely dependent on us – Nigerians – and our collective efforts.

Call it the beginner's guide to nation-building and you wouldn't be far from the truth.

Bobby opines that "it is not the efforts of government (alone) that builds a great nation but rather the thoughts, words and actions of the people." I agree absolutely. The reason why you were born into Nigeria is because you came with a unique solution for an aspect of Nigeria's challenges. There is a place that you were created, empowered and wired to transform and you must find that place.

It is my desire therefore, that as you read this beautifully crafted book, you will let the change begin from within you and find expression without.

That you will stumble upon courage to deliver the future you currently carry. To do everything you can do that you have not yet done and to be everything you can be but have not yet become. That you may ultimately deliver the future and contribute immensely to the realisation of the new Nigeria we all seek.

Deliver the future!
You can. You must. You will.

Fela Durotoye

Introduction

Draw a mental picture of what a developed nation looks like. This is the destination for nation-building.

I feel privileged to be writing a book on nation-building as our nation celebrates 50 years of independence. The dreams of our founding fathers – and that of Nigerians – are yet to be realized but we must be grateful for whatever progress we have made.

Nigeria is a nation with great potentials due to her abundant human and mineral resources. I am constantly amazed at how much resources God endowed one nation with and, I guess, it is this sense of amazement that has led to a deep frustration among Nigerians (and foreigners) since the resources has not turned into wealth for her people. Consequently, we are a poor nation with angry citizens.

Our anger is so visible that any gathering of two or more Nigerians witnesses an intense discussion about the state of our nation and the tempo of such discussions are normally quite aggressive. But the question usually asked, especially by foreigners, is, what would we, Nigerians, do about it?

That question has rarely been properly addressed because what seems to dominate our thoughts, discussions and actions, is criticisms of our government. At best, we propose how to effect change in our political leadership. This reflects that most Nigerians think our main problem is lack of credible political leadership. This view is further supported by those who would state that the defaults in our colonial history are the genesis of our problems. These defaults – starting with the amalgamation of Northern and Southern Nigeria in 1914 – have resulted in rivalry amongst ethnic groups which has impeded opportunities for our best brains and replaced merit with nepotism.

It is hard to dispute this strongly held view. However, since 1999, we have witnessed a democratic dispensation where we decide who our leaders are and for the first time in our history, we have had 12 years of civilian regime (1999-2011) without interruptions by the military. In the process, we witnessed the first transfer of power from one civilian administration to another in May 29th 2007.

Irrespective of the huge criticism of our electoral processes, we are making some progress in the political scene. No matter how limited, we have seen some positive developments in our executive and legislative arm of government — federal, state and local. With the continuous stability of the democratic dispensation, we will hopefully see more positive developments as Nigerians gain further understanding of how the democratic process works and the power it bestows on the people (both of which comes by experience). In fact, a few places have recorded some measure of credible elections, where the people spoke with their votes and several of those elected have come up with exciting blueprints of what they intend to achieve. So, on that note, one can say the Nigerian 'ship' is sailing on even though at a slow pace and with a lot of turbulences.

However, I view our problem differently. If we consider c redible elections as the solution to our problem, the question then becomes what if the person we elect into office goes on to loot the treasury like those who rigged into office? We know credible elections do not necessarily translate into credible candidates and even when it does produce a credible candidate, we know such candidate is weighted down by the challenges and demands of the political system (godfathers, huge campaign funds and support groups needed for political survival and relevance).

Also, if we consider that major infrastructure development is our solution, the question then is what happens: where the roads, schools, power stations, hospitals, water projects etc., which were built, with inflated contracts in most cases, falls apart within a few months; where death on the new roads is comparable to that on the roads when they were bad; where newly built schools have teachers with divided attention due to their private practice or other businesses; where there are hospitals with new structure and equipments but poor services from staff.

I can go on and on but the point I am trying to make is simple: whatever progress we seek to make in our democratic dispensation will be interrupted by the deterioration of the quality of the Nigerian, and this is where the political leadership originates from. We are fast becoming a people with no values – style (perception) and little or no substance (reality). No wonder our nation is one that seems good at producing laws, slogans (vision 2020, 7 point agenda, etc.), economic blueprints, panel of enquiries and white papers, political groups, NGOs, etc., but little or no implementation or enforcement. Effective implementation or enforcement requires the involvement of not only the government but a critical mass of the people. Today, Nigerians are said to be one of the most lawless set of people and this is not limited to those based in Nigeria, but it includes those who live in lawful societies. For the majority of us, the country Nigeria exist only as our mini-nation (me, myself and I) which is what we look out for and serve with all our might. As long as this continues, we cannot hope for visionary leadership and dependable followership which are products of a communal nation.

We all agree that God has endowed Nigeria with potential for greatness but that would remain a dream if Nigerians do not become great. Most of us call Nigeria a failed state and without knowing it, we've called ourselves a failed people. It is us all that make our nation great or failed.

I have come to the conclusion that our greatest need is the reengineering of the Nigerian and by that I mean, transforming the mindset of the Nigerian from being self-focused to nation-focused (from our individual mini-nations to one communal nation). We have fought as individuals for too long and have very little to show for it. It is, therefore, time to start fighting as a nation. The benefits that will accrue to us all will affect all facets of our nation, not just the political scene.

Nation-building is that concept which shifts responsibility for Nigeria from the government to the citizens. It views the daily activities of citizens as more important than activities of the people in government. With a greater number of us being the followership, our impact will be much greater than that of those in government. Bill Halamandaris in his book, The Heart of America, observed that, "Long-term change, the only kind that can be sustained, always come from the bottom up". That change comes from the masses and will result in change in the political leadership. But we must show leadership at the 'bottom level'.

The change needed in our political, social and economic realms is in us and starts with how we live our lives. This new mindset first looks inward into our lives and how we conduct ourselves, then outwards. It looks at how our values are expressed in our roles as parents, children, neighbours, colleagues, employers, employees and citizens. In essence, it translates a big idea or concept into simple steps we can apply in our daily lives that would ensure our transformation and that of those around us.

I am convinced that this is how best we can build our nation and I do hope that by reading this book, you too will become as convinced and together we can implement the necessary changes in and through our lives.

This book is solution focused and like one of American's founding fathers, Thomas Paine, said, so I also say, "I offer nothing more than simple facts, plain arguments, and common sense."

chapter one

What is Nation-Building?

Watch your thoughts, for they become words.
Watch your words, for they become actions.
Watch your actions, for they become habits.
Watch your habits, for they become character.
Watch your character, for it becomes your destiny.
UNKNOWN

The foundation of what this book sets out to achieve is found in what I believe nation-building is. But before I lay out my definition, let's look at some common definitions of nation-building. According to Wikipedia, "Nation-building refers to the process of constructing or structuring a national identity using the power of the state. This process aims at the unification of the people or peoples within the state so that it remains politically stable and viable in the long run. It can involve the use of propaganda or major infrastructure development to foster social harmony and economic growth."

It has also been referred to as the efforts of newly-independent nations — notably the nations of Africa — to mould what had been colonial territories, carved up by colonial powers without regard to ethnic or boundaries, into viable and coherent national entities. It includes the creation of superficial national paraphernalia such as flags, anthems, national days, national stadiums, national airlines, national languages, and national myths.

Nation-building has also been defined as the efforts by a

foreign power to construct or install the institutions of a national government, according to a model that may be more familiar to the foreign power. A good example of this can be seen in the United States (US) and their Allies invasion of Iraq in 2003. James Payne, a renowned political scientist with the Independent Institute in Washington DC, defines it as, "the use of ground troops to support a deliberative effort to create a democracy." (Payne, 2004).

Agreeing with the above definition, James Dobbins in his study for RAND Corporation defined nation-building as, "the use of armed force in the aftermath of a conflict to underpin an enduring transition to democracy." James Dobbins (2003). This report looked at how American military power was used to impose democracy in Germany, Japan, Somalia, Haiti, Bosnia, Kosovo and Afghanistan.

I like the definition of Valerian Cardinal Gracias who uses the term 'National Development' for nation-building, "National development does not consist merely in economic progress but means increasing possibility for all, of living a fully human life on the physical (material), cultural, spiritual levels. It also implies the growing ability of a nation as whole to take its rightful place in the international field, economically, politically, culturally, i.e., to function with a proper degree of autonomy and prestige" (Gracias, 1967).

My Definition

Since this book is not a scholarly work, my definition is simple and it is common sense. Nation-building refers to the creation of thoughts, expression of words and participation in actions that are focused on the nation rather than self. Such thoughts, words and actions, are aimed at building and sustaining a nation that is developed in every sense of the word — economically, politically, socially and spiritually. The result would be a strong and durable foundation and structure for future generations. By nation we mean, a large body of people associated with a particular territory. This large body of people is a collection of communities and the community is the coming together of families. Therefore, in simpler terms, nation-building is about those thoughts, words and actions focused on our families and communities.

We all agree on the importance of constructing or structuring a national identity through the power of the state and the undertaking of major infrastructural development using the resources of the state as part of nation-building. However, I believe these are effects and not causes of nation-building because nation-building is much more than the view that those with the apparatus of the state (the Government), are the only builders of the nation. My definition shifts the focus from the people in government and places responsibility on the citizenry — where the people in government originate from. We are all builders of the nation and the foundation for building rest on the thoughts, words and actions we initiate and implement. I make bold to say that primarily it is not the efforts of government that builds a great nation but rather the thoughts, words and actions of the people. A nation is built or developed to the extent of how much nation-focus thoughts her citizens possess, the words they express and the actions they undertake.

To stress this definition further, I believe the lack of basic amenities, law and order, rule of law, political, economic and social stability, growth etc., are not primarily the result of poor leadership in government but rather the lack of nation-focused citizens, better put, nation-builders. For out of nation-focused citizens will come nation-focused leaders, after all, our leaders do not drop from outer space but are a product of the citizenry (our families and communities).

Let's look at the definition in more details:

Creation of Thoughts

All that you accomplish or fail to accomplish with your life is the direct result of your thoughts. You are today where your thoughts have brought you; you will be tomorrow where your thoughts take you.
JAMES ALLEN

To say nation-building is first the creation of thoughts, is to acknowledge the power of thoughts as the starting point for any form of development. The state of any nation is a reflection of the citizens' thoughts. Therefore, for nation-building to occur in Nigeria, we need to first address our thoughts. Former US president, Dwight Eisenhower, said "Whatever America hopes to bring to pass in the world must first happen in the heart of America". I believe this applies to Nigeria as well and it means, whatever we desire to see in our nation must first happen in our thoughts.

What are thoughts?

Our thoughts are largely buried just beneath our conscious awareness and contain a massive collection of information (beliefs, values, attitudes, opinions, etc.) that we have accumulated through the years and stored away in our minds. We use these thoughts to give meaning to our outer social, physical, and spiritual world. It must be noted that our family, community and school, plays a key role in determining the type of information that we accumulate (which means, our environment has a huge influence on nation-building). Our thoughts are our first 'action' and it determines the words we speak and the real action we take. So, we need to create nation-focused thoughts and not self-centred thoughts. Reason being, the product of nation-focused thoughts will be nation-focused words and nation-focused actions. We can, therefore say our actions are really an interpretation of our thoughts.

To build a great nation, we must have citizens who believe in the country (irrespective of how she was created) and further believe that: Nigeria is not a built nation and the onus is on us to build it; Nigeria can be — and will be — a great nation; each of us have the ability and the capacity to build and sustain a great nation with our specific God given talent; Nigeria belongs to all of us and we are responsible for her development; we cannot separate our individual dreams and aspiration from that of the country; sacrifices are required from us and they will yield the desired result, a developed nation; our values, attitudes and opinions towards the nation must and can change.

Change in our thoughts will not automatically solve the problem but it is an essential starting point because our perspective of the problem would change. When that change in perspective occurs, we would no longer be problem focused, seeing the problem as impossible, but rather, we will become solution focused, identifying the solutions that we can offer individually and communally.

We can, therefore, say our thoughts are primarily responsible for the development of our nation. John Gardner, a former secretary in the US administration said, "Every year millions of Americans come to Washington to visit our national shrines — the Lincoln Memorial, The Washington Monument, the Capitol. But the spirit of the nation does not reside in these physical structures. It is in the minds of the citizens who come to look at the structures. That is where a vital society begins; and, if it ends, that is where it will end"

For our nation to be built, emphasis must be placed on the environment that determines these thoughts to ensure that we create nation-focused thoughts. Such environment is transformed by the imbibing the nation-building core values which will be discussed in chapter three of this book.

Expression of Words

Words have a magical power. They can bring either the greatest happiness or deepest despair; they can transfer knowledge from teacher to student; words enable the orator to sway his audience and dictate its decisions. Words are capable of arousing the strongest emotions and prompting all men's actions.
SIGMUND FREUD

Nation-building is also the expression of words. Words reveal the thoughts we have and determine the actions we take. Therefore, we must utter words that reflect the sort of nation we believe we can and will build and sustain. Laura Esquivel stated in her novel, Swift as Desire, "Desires and words go hand in hand ... they are moved by the same intention to join together, to communicate, to establish bridges between people, whether they are spoken or written." The Holy Scriptures sums it up thus, "Out of the abundance of the heart, the mouth speaks" (Matthew 12:34).

Words create impressions, images and expectations: they build psychological connections or barriers: they reflect or influence how we think. Since thoughts determine actions, the words we speak are a connection between what we think and what we do. Therefore, our words have creative powers enabling our nation-focused thoughts manifest into nation-focused actions. It is true that Nigerians talk a lot about the problems in the nation but it is an indication of our problem based approach to our national issues instead of solution based approach. The problem based approach is a product of the self-focused thoughts we have about our nation. It is common to hear Nigerians declare that Nigeria is a useless country and will not change in this generation but we don't realize that we are calling ourselves useless. So, we see that words reflects the values and beliefs we hold in our thoughts

With our nation-focused words, we can remove the atmosphere of negativity in our nation and replace it with an atmosphere of realistic faith. Building of a nation can only occur in an atmosphere of faith as people will only build what they believe in and destroy what they don't believe in.

Participation in Action

The world is a dangerous place, not because of those who do evil, but because of those who look on and do nothing.
ALBERT EINSTEIN

Understanding and learning to consciously and intentionally implement the power of our thoughts and our words is a vital and necessary component for achieving and experiencing our most sought after dreams and desires for our nation. That is what action is, implementation. Without trying to place too much emphasis on actions, because without the right thoughts and words, there can be no right actions, it still has to be said that action is the crucial element in nation-building. Yes, action is crucial and the final jigsaw in nation-building because it is what makes the greatest impact. I see nation-focused thoughts and words as seeds, while nation-focused actions are the fruits.

I call it 'Mass Participation in Action" because the emphasis is on all citizens (from all age group, ethnicity, sex and status) undertaking individual and collective nation-focused actions. Dele Cole, a former Nigerian ambassador to Brazil, said in an article in The Punch Newspaper, "The greatest asset of Nigeria is not oil but its people and their irrepressible energy". You're not likely to find many Nigerians or foreigners who doubt our 'irrepressible energy'. With nation-focused thoughts and words, this will be harnessed into actions that will build our nation. When we see Nigerians actively participating in positive actions, we see the fruits of positive thoughts and words and such actions will develop into positive habits and the habits will in turn develop into excellent character.

Nigeria is not a developed nation, this we must accept. Nation-building implies that people are doing the building intentionally, that is, constructing a lasting 'edifice' on purpose. Building requires action and according to Colleen C Barrett, "When it comes to getting things done, we need fewer architects and more bricklayers." To build a great Nigeria, there is desperate need for 'bricklayers' (nation-builders), every citizen who will use their God given skills, talent and opportunities to put into action their nation-focused thoughts and words. How we undertake mass participation in action will be treated in more details in chapter four.

chapter two

Why Nation-Building?

There are two great days in a person's life – the day we are born and the day we discover why.
WILLIAM BARCLAYS

After establishing what we refer to as Nation-building, in this chapter, we shall focus on the why question. Voltaire said "Judge a person by their questions, rather than their answers." The most important question is the why question because knowing how has limited merit but people who make greater impact are those who understand why. William Barclay made what I consider to be a fundamental statement when he stated, "There are two great days in a person's life – the day we are born and the day we discover why." That is how important the why question is.

The objective of this chapter is to put first things first: Focus on the why (motive) before tackling the how (process). Reason being that if the why question is properly addressed, then the 'how to' yields the right result. If our actions as a nation have been defective, then we must give special attention to the *why* question. Knowing what nation-building is, is not sufficient enough. The *why* provides understanding and we are liberated and empowered by what we understand.

With the number of books, seminars, workshops, articles and other efforts focused on how to change Nigeria, how to become a success and how to become good leaders, one wonders why we have achieved little progress. Many world renowned leadership gurus have visited Nigeria and we have some great leadership gurus of our own, not to mention that a good number of our people have an amiable library of leadership resources. Those are not bad in themselves but something is lacking – the motive.

We have to ask – fully understand – why we need good leaders before learning how to become one. In the same vein, we have to ask, not assume, why we need basic amenities like light, water, road, healthcare, schools, etc., before focusing on how and what should be provided.

When we take a step back and address the *why* question, we focus attention on evaluating and appropriately addressing the *what* question (our thoughts, words and actions), in readiness for the *how* question. So, it is imperative that we must first address the *why* before the *how*. Here is a simple illustration:

When a man decides he wants to build a house, he must first ask why he wants to build the house before he determines how he will achieve it. He must establish in his mind what purpose the house will serve in the short, medium and long term. He may identify the need to provide a family home, an asset for his children, savings on rental cost, asset to provide collateral for investment, a build to let investment, etc. It is what he has establishes as his motive that will determine the building plan (design, budget, quality of materials, completion date, etc). With an established purpose in mind, accompanied by expression of words and actions, his family and friends will understand what he seeks to achieve and may play an active role in assisting him to achieve and sustain it both in his lifetime and long after he is gone.

It is the *why* that creates of vision in our minds of what a developed Nigeria will look like and how we and our children will live in that era. We must consistently dream of life in a developed Nigeria while we work to actualize it.

In our definition, I stated that nation-building is the creation of thoughts, the expression of words and the participation in actions. To understand why we must create nation-focused thoughts, express nation-focused words and undertake nation-focused actions, lets look at two key *why* questions. I believe every Nigerian must be confronted with these two questions:

a. Why should we build our nation?

b. Why is nation-building the key?

Before we discuss why nation-building (nation focused thoughts, words and actions) is the key to building our nation, we must first establish why we should build our nation.

Why should we build our nation?

This is the fundamental question we must all ask ourselves and not just once but everyday of our lives, especially when confronted with huge sacrifices for the sake of our nation. When we remind ourselves of the benefits that would accrue to us and our children (generations to come), we will become and remain committed to the demands that nation-building places on us. In some cases, the demands of nation-building may cost us our lives and/or that of our families. No nation has ever been built without the blood, tears, toil and sweat of her people.

We have had several programmes by government and different organisations to raise patriotic zeal amongst Nigerians or rebrand our country. However, we have to take a step back and address why we bother (what is in it for me?), to enable significant and sustained efforts. Only when the motives are accepted and established in our heart would we be willing to open ourselves to changes in our thoughts, words and actions.

It is not enough to know what is needed but the motivation to consistently do what is needed is essential. That motivation will help overcome the fears of the sacrifices required as we become transformed by the nation-building core values. A 19th Century philosopher, Friedrich Nietzsche, stated, "He who has a why can endure any how". Here lies the essence of this question and until we fully digest this question – we all should —we would not be ready to become nation-builders.

Here are some key reasons why, I believe, we should build our nation:

We are the only builders of the nation

A Chinese proverb says "Rise and fall of a nation rest with every one of its citizens". We the citizens of Nigeria are the builders of this nation. At the 2005 G8 Summit in Gleneagles, the former British Prime Minister, Tony Blair, made a profound statement when he said, "The only people that will change Africa ultimately are Africans". No! we do not need the British or Americans to come build our nation, though we can learn from how they built theirs. Despite their continuous efforts and huge resources invested in Nigeria, international organizations or charities from Western nations cannot develop our nation for us.

This nation belongs to us — I repeat, *this nation belongs to us* — and the onus to build her rest upon us. It is not the years of military rule or years of corrupt civilian administration, we must hold responsible but ourselves. We are the builders and not just our leaders. We must build the nation through our thoughts, words and actions. To do so, we must accept the responsibility placed on each of us, as builders of the nation. As American writer Richard Bach noted, "If it's never our fault, we can't take responsibility for it. If we can't take responsibility for it, we'll always be its victim."

The current state of our nation is the fault of all Nigerians and only we, Nigerians, are the builders of this nation. God and generations to come will hold us responsible.

Don't build, don't inhabit

If we do not build or develop our nation, we can not inhabit a developed nation. Building the nation is for our own benefit and that of our children. We are the first beneficiaries.

Every Nigerian desires a nation that has law and order, rule of law, well developed infrastructure, good healthcare services, relevant and effective educational system, stable and diversified economy, well entrenched democracy, and so on. These are the fruits of a nation that has been developed. It is the fruits we will reap if we dedicate our all to developing the nation, instead of focusing on ourselves. The true measure of nation's development is not wealth of individuals but the quality of life of the people. *The nation prospers, we prosper. The nation collapses, we collapse.* The American Speaker and Author, Jim Rohn remarked that, "Whatever good things we build end up building us."

Best Guarantee for our Children

The best guarantee of a better tomorrow for our children is building the nation today. As important as good education and material assets are, they are no guarantee of a better quality of life for our children. It is a developed nation that will ensure that our children, irrespective of social status, will have a society that encourages the expression of and rewards talent; ensures the protection of life and property; protects the freedom of movement, association and speech; provides and sustains good infrastructure; highly esteems the rule of law, etc.

How effective or secured is a child trained in one of the world's best educational institutions if he or she has to come back to work and live in a nation with poor transportation network and standard, low level of security, low level of human capital, political instability and lack of law and order? An undeveloped nation affects all of us and not just the poor and less privileged. Our children will be guaranteed a better quality of life if we sacrifice for the sake of the nation today.

In the words of former Wisconsin Governor and co-founder of Earth Day, "The ultimate test of man's conscience may be his willingness to sacrifice something today for future generations whose words of thanks will not be heard" (Gaylord Nelson 1970).

Legacy

A key similarity in the developed nations of today is their rich history of men, women and movements that contributed immensely towards building the nation. It is these past sacrifices that creates a deep sense of patriotism and inspires generations to come, who would protect the ideals that made those nations great. We do not just build our nation for the benefits we shall receive now but for the rich legacies we give to generations to come, providing them a nation to be proud of and a nation to die for. Building a nation surely does requires a lot of sacrifices but it creates a rich history that sustains the culture of sacrifices.

The United States of America has a rich history of people who made sacrifices that are talked about by her people everyday. The Patriots, as they are called, still stir up patriotism in Americans hundreds of years after they were gone. Americans do not only talk about their patriots or just hold a deep sense of patriotism, but they are motivated to do all they can to protect and preserve what those patriots provided through their sweat and blood. President Obama, like most American leaders, regularly makes references to American patriots. At his inaugural address after taking his presidential oath of office in January 2009, he stated "For us, they packed up their few worldly possessions and travelled across oceans in search of a new life. For us, they toiled in sweatshops and settled the West; endured the lash of the whip and ploughed the hard earth. For us, they fought and died, in places like Concord and Gettysburg, Normandy and Khe Sanh. Time and again these men and women struggled and sacrificed and worked till their hands were raw so that we might live better life. They saw America as bigger than the sum of our individual ambitions, greater than all the differences of birth or wealth or faction."

A people proud of their history are naturally proud of their nation and will be willing to make the required sacrifices to sustain the nation's development. As former British Prime

Minister, Benjamin Disraeli, puts it, "The legacy of heroes is the memory of a great name and the inheritance of a great example."

Sense of fulfilment

The greatest pursue of man is personal fulfilment and true fulfilment is not attained through the acquisition of wealth, money, academic and traditional titles but by the change we make in our society. Here is how Anthony Robbins puts it, "Only those who have learned the power of sincere and selfless contribution experience life's deepest joy: true fulfilment." Since true fulfilment is connected to the changes we make in society, we can conclude that nation-building will deliver that fulfilment. So, when we focus our talents, energy and resources (in thoughts, words and actions) towards building the nation, we do not only build a great nation but achieve life main goal – true fulfilment.

The famous American football Coach, Vince Lombardi, said, "I firmly believe that any man's finest hour, the greatest fulfilment of all that he holds dear, is the moment when he has worked his heart out in a good cause and lies exhausted on the field of battle - victorious" There could be no greater fulfilment for us as a people than to dedicate our all to building and sustaining a great nation.

Answer the Call

God has bestowed upon Nigeria potential, in huge resources (human and material) and has placed a call on each of us to develop the potential into greatness. This call is not on some but on every Nigerian because God works through people to achieve His purpose –not just a few superstars.

Moreover, I believe God intended the greatness of Nigeria to also be for the benefit of the African continent because every time He blesses a person or a people, the purpose is for the recipient to be blessed and to become a blessing to others. That is why our nation has been entrusted with enormous material and human resources. When we expand our vision beyond ourselves and even our nation, we would minimize waste in our time and resources. By building our nation, we are responding to that call to maximize our potential to our suffering continent's benefit. Nigeria's call is to be blessed and to be a blessing. Building Nigeria is our God-given assignment and we will be held accountable for it. Luke 12:48 says "To whom much is given, much is expected".

Taking Back Our Nation

We take control of the destiny of our nation when we decide to build the nation. One of the key signs of an undeveloped nation is the control of that nation by a few and in the process denying the people their freedom. That has been the case with Nigeria and to take control of our nation, we must get involved in building the nation.

The famous South African author and political activist, Alan Paton, once said, "To give up the task of reforming society is to give up one's responsibility as a free man". While Leo F. Buscaglia summed it up thus, "If we wish to free ourselves from enslavement, we must choose freedom and the responsibility this entails". The only way we can become free — free to determine and protect our future — is to rise up and build our nation.

Establish our Dignity

Dignity refers to the state of being worthy of esteem or respect. To establish the dignity of the Nigerian, we must build our nation. According to Albert Einstein, "Not until we dare to regard ourselves as a nation, not until we respect ourselves, can we gain the esteem of others, or rather only then will it come of its own accord". To gain the dignity amongst the committee of nations, we have to regard ourselves as a nation, respect ourselves and build our nation. As quoted, only then will the esteem of others come, the dignity we desire. The others here refer to the committee of nations.

Due to the undeveloped state of our nation, we are noted mainly for our negative activities. Consequently, Nigerians are regularly humiliated in various countries around the world. As we have no dignity in ourselves, we cannot command the respect of others. It is important to note that such humiliation is not limited to ordinary Nigerians but even the so called elites, as long as one is carrying a symbol of our identity and nationality (passport, name, accent, dress code, and the like).

When we build our nation, our citizens will be guaranteed treatment with dignity abroad and not only that, our nation will also be treated with dignity by the international community. This is because a developed nation creates a good image for the people of that nation. With the respect and influence we would command globally, not just in Africa, Nigeria can easily achieve a permanent membership of the United Nations Security Council, play a leading role in the political and economic emancipation of Africa, become a global economic power with political, social and economic influence and earn a bigger role in mediating global crisis.

The dignity of a nation is the dignity of her people and the dignity of a people is the dignity of a nation. This is why we must build our nation.

Why is nation-building the key?

Having understood why we must build our nation, we now must understand why nation-building is the key to building our nation. Besides fully digesting the benefits that could come to us, we also need to fully digest why it has to be nation-building.

Here are some reasons:

Reveals the Root Cause

Whatever we do as a people is determined by the thoughts (beliefs, values, opinions, attitudes) we hold. The heart of our problem as a nation is down to the defects in our thoughts, which determines our words and actions. As stated earlier, our actions are the manifestation of our thoughts. Nation-building holds the key because it shifts the focus from the usual poor leadership, corruption, ethnic agitations, religious crisis, etc (they are effects and not the causes); to the thoughts each Nigerian has about the nation.

Reveals Current State of the Nation

Nation-building shows us where we are currently, what can be attained and makes clear what is required to achieve a developed nation. As we come to terms with the fact that it is our thoughts, words and actions that holds the key, we come to realize that our nation is not developed due to the defects in our thoughts.

It is not possible to fully understand what is required for any building project until a proper realization and acceptance of the current state of affairs. This is crucial. An overview of our actions, as Nigerians, indicates that we believe our nation is developed. If we do not think so: why do we act like people living in developed nations? Our lifestyle is a key example.

Most Nigerians believe that Nigeria is a rich nation but the truth remains, she lacks the qualities of rich nations: first class infrastructure, vibrant and diversified economy, law and order, human capital development, good healthcare and educational systems, etc. While we may have abundant of human and material resources and may have some good revenue from oil, it does not qualify our nation as wealthy in the absence of what we see in rich nations. This is what nation-building establishes. When we accept where we are currently, come to terms with what it means to be a developed nation and the efforts required, we are then prepared to build the nation.

Shifts Responsibility

Nation-building shifts responsibility for building the nation to individuals from just our leaders. This is because it places emphasis on the thoughts, words and actions of each Nigerian, privileged or less privileged, educated or uneducated, employed or unemployed, Christian or Muslim or Atheist, Northerner or Southerner, and so on. No solution can cause the development of any nation without the active participation of the masses. Nation-building places that demand on every citizen of Nigeria.

There is an erroneous idea that, one man can change the destiny of our nation. We call it good leadership. Nation-building debunks that idea because it highlights the fact that no leader can succeed without a people focused on the development of the nation. If the citizens are self-focused, the impact of good leadership will be limited and short term.

No matter how great the leader, we've had some in our nation, they can only start the process by providing guidance and inspiration. An effective followership is required to implement and sustain the ideas of the great leader. As a leader is the servant of the people, he will be required to serve their perceived needs and where he fails to do that, the success of his policies are limited. I believe this is a strong indicator as to why self focused leadership thrives in Nigeria and why the impact of good leaders is limited.

Because nation-building places responsibility on every Nigerian and leadership is primarily about responsibility, we are then all leaders — in our workplace, homes, community, etc. We first lead ourselves and then serve the people around us through our thoughts, words and actions.

Summary

If we are not building the 'communal' nation (Nigeria), we are building the 'individual' nation (ourselves). That means, we are seeking to acquire as much as possible for ourselves, ignoring the community. It is not surprising then that our 'communal' nation is in crisis because the various 'individual' nations are competing against each other to possess whatever is available. This has provided an excellent opportunity for corruption, ethnicity, violence and criminality to thrive. We are created for communal living and that means we are to exist as a community. This is why we need to build our nation and that starts with being nation-focused instead of self-focused.

Why is the bridge that connects the *what* with the *how* and the effective understanding of the *why* means the effectively implementation of the *how*.

chapter three

Nation-Building Core Values

Values provide perspective in the best of times and the worst.
CHARLES GARFIELD

After we have discussed what nation-building really means and addressed why we must build and why nation-building is key, it is necessary to identify the ingredients we must possess to become nation-builders. These ingredients are called Core Values and the foundation for producing nation-focused thoughts, words and actions.

Values are our beliefs, ideals and convictions. They determine what we think, say or how we act, which is why they can transform our thoughts, words and actions from self-focused to nation-focused. It is pertinent to note that we must fully understand what nation-building is and accept why we need to build our nation as that would determine the extent to which we allow these values become part of our lives. A nation that holds these values as a collective belief is a nation with enlightened citizens and a nation with strong spiritual and moral ethics, which are prerequisites for a developed nation.

It is also worth adding that the absence of these core values is a strong indicator of a nation that is not developed. It was through the creation, the communication and the defence of these core values that the American patriots built America and it also provides a guide to how that nation is to be sustained or rebuilt by future generations. Therefore, core values provide the framework that builds a nation and a guide for generations to come on how to sustain a nation's greatness. But again it starts first by understanding what nation-building is and why we must build our nation.

In his book, *The Heart of America: Ten Core Values That Make Our Country Great*, Bill Halamandaris, listed ten core values that built America. Ten values with proven ability to build a world superpower.

America is an excellent nation-building example because it was built by the thoughts, words and actions (sacrifices) of her forefathers (appropriately called the Patriots). I agree with President Lyndon B. Johnson, who claimed that America is the first nation in history of the world to be founded with a purpose. Core values were held as a guiding principle in their effort to build a great America and I am convinced that these same values can provide a key guide in our effort to build a great Nigeria.

It is interesting to note that these values are intertwined; they depend on each other to ensure success in building a nation. It is profound to note that these values that build a great nation are the same values that build an individual (after all, a nation is a community of individuals). This means, these values should first be applied *in* our individual lives before it is applied *through* our lives to the nation. Albert Einstein was quoted as saying "Try not to be a man of success but rather try to become a man of value". This is the key to producing nation-builders and it is people of value that build lasting positive legacy in society.

Compassion Opportunity Responsibility Equality
Valour Ambition Liberty Unity Enterprise Spirituality

Compassion

The value of compassion cannot be over-emphasized. Anyone can criticize. It takes a true believer to be compassionate. No greater burden can be borne by an individual than to know no one cares or understands.

ARTHUR H. STAINBACK

Compassion is a sense of shared suffering, most often combined with a desire to alleviate or reduce such suffering. Bill Halamandaris calls it, man's highest attribute. He went further to state, "Most of even our best instincts have a base side. Love, hope, faith, courage and loyalty can all be corrupted by ego, selfishness, and human frailty, transformed into doubt, fear and hate. True compassion stands alone unyielding."

Its cultivation is considered a primary virtue by the two dominant religions in Nigeria, Islam and Christianity; therefore, there is a strong religious basis for practicing it. It should not be only a religious law or commandment but a core value that is central to our lifestyle and would impact on our social, economic and political system. Compassion is not pity which is what we often practice. Pity focuses on the sufferings of a person. As a result, pity creates a gap or distance which can lead to feelings of alienation, shame and inferiority on the part of the suffering person, and superiority and contempt on the part of the person showing pity. But compassion focuses on and is attentive to the suffering person. Compassion is able to bridge the gap of separation because it is based on the acceptance that we are creatures of God. Dr Martin Luther King Jr. described it thus, "Pity may represent little more than the impersonal concern which prompts the mailing of a check, but true sympathy is the personal concern which demands the giving of one's soul."

"Compassion is anchored in unity and equality and expressed in opportunity and responsibility" (Bill Halamandaris). Therefore, we can say that a nation built on compassion will be a nation where everyone protects each others' rights to be free to live where and how they want and to be free to say what they want and do what they like, within the law and with the attendant responsibility. As Rush Limbaugh puts it, "Telling people to believe in themselves is the ultimate in compassion". Compassion creates a strong community base and that is the foundation for building a nation. A nation is primarily a committee of communities and the display of compassion strengthens the ties between people, families and communities.

According to Bill Halamandaris, "Compassion is the bridge between us. It connects our lives by a thousand sympathetic threads. We all need to find our compassion and find support in the compassion of others. At its essence compassion is the difference in saying 'I am my brother's keeper' and 'I am my brother'" In a society where thousands of people are dying from curable illnesses like malaria in the midst of resources to tackle the problem, compassion is desperately needed. This is just one aspect of our society that highlights the urgent need for a nation that places a premium value on compassion.

Bill Shore, founder of one of America's largest non-profit organization, Share our Strength, stated that during his time on Capitol Hill as a top congressional aide, he learnt that when it comes to helping the poor, money is not enough. "It takes mentoring. It takes working with people. It takes coaching. It takes that type of personal exchange to really turn someone's life around." Compassion is the motivating value for this sort of commitment. We cannot hope to have the nation of our dreams if we are not ready to become a people of compassion, showing deep commitment to our families, friends, neighbours and community. Their development is the development of our nation, so they need our compassion.

Compassion as a core nation-building value, must be studied, practiced, taught and inspired by each and every one of us in our effort to build our nation. Also, churches and mosques must play a leading role in converting compassion from a commandment or law we try to keep into a core value we live by each day. After all, any religion without the expression of compassion by her followers is ineffective as shown in the message behind that biblical parable of the Good Samaritan. (Luke 10:25)

Opportunity

All that is valuable in human society depends upon the opportunity for development accorded the individual.
ALBERT EINSTEIN

A nation is developed to the extent with which her people have the opportunity to express their thoughts, words and talents. America is a superpower today because she is proven to be a land of opportunity. No other nation in modern history has seen tens of millions of immigrants (over 1 million each year in recent years) who have not only made that country their home but have gone on to reach the pinnacle of their chosen venture. A famous American author Thomas Wolfe best describe this when he wrote, "So, then, to every man his chance – to every man, regardless of his birth, his shining, golden opportunity – to every man the right to live, to work, to be himself, and to become whatever thing his manhood and his vision can combine to make him – this, seeker, is the promise of America." That is the essence of the American Dream and we can make it a Nigerian Dream.

Opportunity means a situation, occasion, condition or an environment favourable for attainment of a goal. It is time we see opportunity as a value provided by the people and not the government. It is essential that we express this core value for all. In order to build the nation, we need to imbibe this value into our thoughts and words and implement it with our actions. The result of which, would be a nation that provides limitless possibilities in the pursuit of happiness.

"Opportunity comes from liberty and is made possible by equality. When fed by ambition and sustained by courage, the pursuit of happiness has limitless possibilities" (Bill Halamandaris). With our freedom, we can create opportunities by recognizing that we are equal and by encouraging people to step out in faith to implement their ideas with boldness. Again, this is not a role we should delegate to government where we seek to build our nation.

We all accept that Nigeria is endowed with enormous mineral and human resources but all these will count for nothing if there are no opportunities for all Nigerians to express their abilities. As Napoleon Bonaparte noted "Ability is of little account without opportunity". The combination of our enormous material resources with our huge population should result in a country that produces world renowned giants in banking, oil and gas, sports, entertainment, agriculture, tourism, manufacturing industries, along with world class infrastructure and research institutes. The value we place on opportunity will ensure we attain these and only then can we truly attain our status as the Giant of Africa.

Many may insist that it is the responsibility of the leadership to provide opportunities and that is partially correct. But I reiterate that in an underdeveloped nation (a nation not yet built), it is the masses who must take responsibility and initiative for creating and protecting the opportunities for nation-building. "Opportunity and responsibility go hand-in-hand." (US President Bill Clinton)

We must also note that in every seemingly impossible situation lies an opportunity and therefore, we can say our 'hopeless' situation offers great opportunities. This thought should motivate every nation-builder. When we put our gifts and abilities to use, it creates opportunities and the more we do this, the more the opportunity. The Bible says in Proverbs 18:16, "A man's gift will make room for him and brings him before great men" and Sun Tzu, the ancient Chinese military general, noted, "Opportunities multiply as they are seized". Opportunities for free qualitative and relevant education; opportunities to train and set up any legitimate venture in any part of the country; opportunities to make and pursue career choices; opportunities to vote and be voted for without coercion or intimidation and much more.

Orison Swett Marden was quoted as saying "Don't wait for extraordinary opportunities. Seize common occasions and make them great. Weak men wait for opportunities; strong men make them." When we value opportunity, we will seize whatever occasion, no matter how small, that arises or create them. The education of our children will continue to achieve less result if we don't all begin to value opportunity for all.

This is why we must establish this value in our hearts, practice it, offer it and demand it from others and teach our children and area of influence in words and deeds. When our nation witnesses a surge in the number of citizens who place high value on opportunity, we will be ready to defend our liberties and equality, even with our lives, and remove the boundaries our society places on our pursuit of happiness. The 19th century American poet Ralph Waldo Emerson said "America is another name for opportunity". We too must be able to think it, say it and act it, that Nigeria is another name for opportunity.

Responsibility

Man must cease attributing his problems to his environment, and learn again to exercise his will — his personal responsibility.
ALBERT EINSTEIN

In the second chapter, we had identified that nation-building shifts the responsibility for building the nation from the leaders to the people; Hence, responsibility is a core value required to build our nation. Responsibility means a state of being responsible, accountable or answerable. Concerning our nation, responsibility is identifying the true state of our nation, that it has not been built, accepting that we are responsible for its current state, accepting what is required to bring change, and accepting our responsibility to use our resources to generate that positive change to the best of our ability.

Former US President, Herbert C. Hoover, stated, "But a large responsibility rests directly upon our citizens." So, we can declare that the responsibility for building and sustaining a great Nigeria rest directly upon us the citizens and not on Aso Rock and the various Government Houses. In the end, we are not only responsible for our own actions but also for the actions of those who work for us and that include our civic and political leaders.

Responsibility states that we have to be what we want in our nation. According to Mahatma Ghandi, "Be the change you want to see in the world". Peaceful if we want peace; honest, principled and transparent if we want a corrupt free society; law abiding if we want a nation with law and order; tax payers if we want basic amenities to be provided.

It is in this sense we have to view Education. Education of our citizens is not only the responsibility of the government but also that of the community, parents and every individual. This means, we accept responsibility to ensure that we become educated and ensure the education of others, for the sake of building and sustaining a developed nation. An educated nation will benefit all citizens (both the privileged and under-privileged).

While there is a strong call for Nigerians to hold their government accountable, it must be said that this cannot be properly achieved if we don't first make ourselves accountable or responsible for the nation. Responsibility is primarily making ourselves accountable to other Nigerians, including our leaders, and holding other Nigerians accountable to us.

According to US President Dwight D. Eisenhower, "The true slogan of democracy is not 'Let the government do it, but rather let's do it ourselves'". Bill Halamandaris adds that responsibility is connected to liberty, "Responsibility is the essence of a free man's life. We are free to the degree we accept responsibility; we lose freedom and liberty to the degree we abdicate our responsibility or let other act for us". This simply means, if we do not take responsibility for our nation and create the society we desire, someone else will and their desire may likely not tally with ours. The current state of our nation is an excellent example of this.

Responsibility is a unique value which brings contentment, character, integrity, discipline to the self and service to others. It also creates a sense of community because responsible people know they have something worthwhile to offer. A responsible person teaches by his actions and in the process inspires others. This is why a truly responsible person is a creator of positive change and a nation-builder.

Responsibility is the fuel that propels thoughts into nation-focused action. It is not enough to have great thoughts about Nigeria as that on its own cannot transmit into actions. But when we have responsibility as a core value, realizing we are responsible for our nation, we are compelled to take nation-focused actions, irrespective of the cost. The renowned German theologian and key opponent of Hitler, Dietrich Bonheoffer, before he was hanged by Nazis wrote, "Action springs not from thought, but from a readiness for responsibility." With responsibility, we will identify opportunities, find the commitment to move into action and the discipline to sustain our efforts.

The absence of the responsibility in our nation has given rise to the focus on style (perception) rather than substance (reality) and this is a reflection of the poor state of our spirituality. We have a society that has a perception of what success or status is, that is determined by what we do, how much we earn, what we look like, what we wear, what we have, cars we drive or titles we acquired (religious, traditional or academic). Style focuses on maintaining an image by acquiring possessions: titles, houses, cars, etc. While substance focuses on significance: character, integrity, courage and humility. It is a responsible citizenry that would break the grip of style on our people and produce a people of substance, people who know their worth before God and express that in daily living. With the nation-building value of Spirituality (to be discussed later in this chapter), we recognize or are reminded that we are all responsible to God for what He has entrusted to us: gifts, abilities, experiences, families, communities, resources — both human and mineral — and the nation. This is the foundation of responsibility.

Equality

Equal rights for all, special privileges for none
THOMAS JEFFERSON

According to Bill Halamandaris, "Equality is the keystone of democracy. From it flows liberty, opportunity and responsibility". Thomas Jefferson, one the founders of the US constitution, puts equality before life, liberty and pursuit of happiness in the opening statement of the American Declaration of Independence, "We hold these truths to be self-evident, that all men are created equal, that they are endowed by their Creator with certain unalienable rights, that among these are life, liberty and the pursuit of happiness."

What is equality? It simply means the state of being equal in quantity, measure, value or status. Article One of the United Nations Declaration of Human Rights states that "All human beings are born free and equal in dignity and rights". Though it has been a key source of controversy in America's history, it can still be argued that it is the dominant value or concept amongst Americans and has made the most significant contribution in making that nation what it is today.

As a nation-building value, equality is not about material condition but rather the frame of mind and attitude. It is a value that must first be exhibited from within — our thoughts — and then reflected without — our words and actions. This simply means that all Nigerians must first believe that we are all equals, whether from the north, south, east or west and irrespective of religious and educational background. We must treat fellow Nigerians as equals and fight against inequality in the society especially against the less privileged.

A society that does not value equality of its citizens is frail and cannot sustain itself indefinitely, without the degeneration of its social fabric which inevitably leads to massive resentment of the government and eventually social unrest. This describes the current state of our nation.

To build this nation, we must confront this 'us' versus 'them' mentality. The attitude of superiority, mostly amongst the major ethnic groups, and of inferiority, mostly amongst the minority ethnic groups, exhibited by one ethnic group toward another must be eradicated. After all, we are all human beings, all interconnected and each has problems (both peculiar and common). It has to be said again that every Nigerian should incorporate the frame of mind and attitude that firstly we are equal to any other Nigerian (any human being) and secondly, other Nigerians are equal to us.

When we hold equality as a core value for our lives and for our nation, it will create a society that is free, with equal opportunities and, responsible and compassionate citizens. It is these values that builds and sustains a great nation.

Valour

A nation or civilization that continues to produce soft-minded men purchases its own spiritual death on the instalment plan.
MARTIN LUTHER KING, JR.

According to the Webster dictionary, "Valour is the strength of mind (or spirit) in regards to danger; that quality which enables a man to encounter danger with firmness; personal bravery; courage; prowess; intrepidity." Valour is a core nation-building value because it exhibits the key qualities of bravery, courage, prowess, persistency amongst citizens of a nation. Valour is not limited to courage in the context of danger or acts of bravery and heroism but also includes acts of compassion and responsibility. According to Bill Halamandaris, "Valour sustains enterprise and ambition, the foundation of the free enterprise society. It seizes opportunity, creates success and is the backbone of liberty."

We need the spirit of valour to enable us do whatever is required, irrespective of the cost, with firm commitment to however long it takes, in our fight against injustice, defence of civil rights and liberty, the harness of opportunities, the pursue and attainment of ambition, the exhibition of unrestrained compassion and the accountability and responsibility to one another.

Founder of the US Democratic Party and 7th US President, Andrew Jackson, stated, "You must pay the price if you wish to secure the blessing." Valour enables us pay that price required to secure the blessings of a developed nation

The importance of valour as a value that builds a nation can be seen in the history of any great nation. Such history is rich with countless acts of bravery and heroism in the face of danger and in ordinary daily living. It is this rich history that gives these nations e.g., America a deep sense of pride in themselves and commands a high degree of respect from the committee of nations. Here lies a key benefit to a nation that holds valour as a value amongst her people. Therefore, to build a great nation, we must seek to identify with, cultivate and exhibit valour as a value in every Nigerian. We can and will take back the destiny of our nation from the so called cabal when we become a nation of valour.

Former US President, Richard Nixon, famously stated, "We cannot live a full life unless we have a purpose bigger than ourselves. We all cannot expect to be great philosophers, scientists, statesmen or business leaders. But we must always seek to reach up and reach out to achieve our full potential. Some of the most heroic lives are lived by those who cope with tragedy, adversity and the daily drudgery of life, and rise above it. It is a mistake to assume we can ever achieve perfection, But it is an even greater mistake to cease trying. Without risk there will be neither success or failure. As Thomas Aquinas observed: 'If the primary aim of a captain were to preserve his ship, he would keep it in the port forever.''

The pre-colonial and colonial history of Nigeria has spots of valour which does provide some indication that we can become a people of valour. However, valour is required amongst the majority of our people and not just by a few heroes. This value has to be applied in our individual lives and then in our families, communities and nation. We need the value of valour in every Nigerian to seize the opportunities available to build for our children a great nation. Our history must become one rich with countless acts of bravery and courage. Nothing will change unless we confront it with valour and the presence of other core nation-building values will easily encourage this value.

Ambition

Without ambition one starts nothing ... .
RALPH WALDO EMERSON

Ambition can be defined as an eager or strong desire to accomplish something and the willingness to strive for its attainment. Anyone that has ever created anything, given this world any value, or simply aspired to greater heights, had a certain ambitious quality. I am sure many who had their secondary school and university education in Nigeria will remember the phrase NFA (No Future Ambition) which was used to describe students with little or no interest in their studies. The result was such students were either expelled or took a longer time to complete their studies. Pearl Bailey, a popular American Entertainer, once said, "A man without ambition is dead". So also, a nation is dead if filled with citizens without ambition but alive when majority of her citizens are full of ambition and pursue its attainment with valour.

Ambition as a core nation-building value, will create a people with an increased desire to achieve or attain their aspirations and in the process, remove predetermined societal boundaries. The end result will not only be accomplishments, accolades, material benefits but it would also create an atmosphere of opportunity, enterprise and liberty. That is the quality of a developed nation.

According to Bill Halamandaris, "Ambition seeks opportunity and thrives on liberty." It is ambition that exploits an opportunity where it exists or creates an opportunity where it does not exist and it is the pursuant of it [ambition] that places a demand on liberty. On the other hand, over ambition has negative impact on an individual and a nation, especially when viewed as pursuance of power or material possession. But this is easily rectified when we remember that ambition is the strong desire to accomplish something that will make our nation better. We must therefore focus our ambition on the nation and not on ourselves, and the result would be beneficial to us, our families and our community.

Also, to ensure proper checks and balances, it is essential for ambition to sit alongside other core values like liberty, equality, responsibility, spirituality and compassion. We must create a country where we are 100% committed to pursuing our legitimate ambition and are also 100% in support of the ambition of others. That would be the evidence of a developed nation

Liberty

Liberty is to the collective body, what health is to every individual body.
Without health no pleasure can be tasted by man; without liberty, no happiness
can be enjoyed by society.
THOMAS JEFFERSON

According to the Webster dictionary Liberty is, "The state of being free, the power to do as one pleases, freedom from despotic control, and the power of choice" Liberty is not only the power but it is also the right to act, believe or express oneself as one pleases. In its original Latin form, the word means free and that means Liberty is also known as freedom. That power and right of freedom includes freedom of religion, freedom of speech, freedom of association and all personal freedoms required to ensure the full legitimate expression of man. According to Aristotle, "The basis of a democratic state is liberty."

This core value must be vigorous pursued by every Nigerian. We will build and sustain a great nation when we don't only pursue freedom for ourselves but equally fight for the freedom of others. This is how Clarence Darrow puts it, "You can protect your liberties in this world only by protecting the other man's freedom. You can be free only if I am free." This is supported by Bill Halamandaris who stated that "Like love, liberty is one of the things you cannot have unless you are willing to share it with others." I believe the extent of our development as a nation is tied to the extent of ours and our neighbour's freedom.

It is this core value that would provide the support or opportunity for the full development of every Nigerian, intellectually, materially, spiritually and morally, which is how our nation will be built. However, liberty has to be checked by equality, compassion, spirituality and responsibility. Friedrich A. Hayek stated that, "Liberty not only means that the individual has both the opportunity and the burden of choice; it also means that he must bear the consequences of his actions ... Liberty and responsibility are inseparable." Bill Halamandaris adds that, "Liberty provides the opportunity to fulfil our ambitions, but it must be balanced by equality and our respect for equal rights of others."

It must be made clear that as part of the nation-building process, the core value of liberty will have to be fiercely fought for, with Valour, to attain it for all Nigerians and to preserve it for future generations. That fight is not undertaken by government but by all Nigerians. This is how Martin Luther King Jr. puts it, "Freedom is never voluntarily given by the oppressor: it must be demanded by the oppressed."

Not only do values such as compassion, responsibility, equality and spirituality help check liberty but they also lighten the weight of the demand for liberty.

Unity

There are no problems we cannot solve together, and very few that we can solve by ourselves.
LYNDON B. JOHNSON

Unity is an essential value that builds a nation. No better way to put it than the way the bible puts it, "Behold, how good and how pleasant it is for brethren to dwell together in unity". Unity is defined as the state of being united or in agreement. It is also denotes a combining of all the parts, elements and individuals into an effective whole.

Since the creation of our nation, many Nigerians have declared the forced marriage of the northern and southern protectorates to form Nigeria as a mistake and a failure. However, to build a great nation we need to look beyond our past and focus on how we can use what we have to create a better future for our children. Our thinking should reflect the thinking of US President, Lyndon B. Johnson, who stated, "We come to reason, not to dominate. We do not seek to have our way, but to find a common way."

To enable this value, we need to draw on other core values such as compassion, responsibility, equality, liberty and spirituality. Our compassion for all Nigerians irrespective of ethnic or religious background through the acceptance of responsibility, along with the defence of the liberties of all, with the mindset that we are all of equal value and worth before God is what will ensure we hold unity as a value. The obvious result is the building of a great nation that will benefit all groups including ourselves and our children. After all, "United we stand, divided we fall".

A critical overview of our nation will indicate that no particular ethnic or religious group is developed and all are suffering the effects of underdevelopment. Therefore, we all have the same interest and need each other to develop and build our nation. Greatness of an individual or a nation is born out of unity.

Unity builds families; united families build strong communities; strong communities produce and sustain a united and developed nation. As Bill Halamandaris stated in his book, *The Heart of America*, "Everyone is needed. Everyone can contribute. Individually, we may only have a small piece of puzzle but each of us has at least one piece, and every piece is essential" He further emphasised that, "Community comes when people see hope where there is fear and decide to join hands, linking themselves with others in a common cause. Community comes when people decide not to ignore a problem or run away, but to reinforce each other and fight apathy and despair. Community comes when we realize nothing of real value can be accomplished alone"

We must be reminded that in our national pledge we swore to defend the unity of Nigeria. Also, unity is the last word of the first stanza of our national anthem and also part of our national motto: Peace and Unity, Strength and Progress.

For our pledge, motto and anthem to have relevance, we must accept unity as a core nation-building value. To imbibe this value, we must shift focus from ourselves to our nation and that would remove the internal conflicts that denies us unity within ourselves. When we resolve this conflict and become united internally, we can express this value to others.

Enterprise

No enterprise can exist for itself alone. It ministers to some great need, it performs some great service, not for itself, but for others; or failing therein, it ceases to be profitable and ceases to exist.
CALVIN COOLIDGE

Enterprise is defined as the boldness or readiness in undertaking, adventurous spirit or ingenuity. It is the willingness to undertake new ventures or initiative. According to Bill Halamandaris, "If ambition is desire, enterprise is action. Enterprise is work, particularly any task that is difficult, complicated or risky. Enterprise is the willingness to step out into the unknown with faith and confidence".

It is the spirit of enterprise that enables a person to risk all to achieve ambition by exploiting opportunity. A great nation is built when enterprise becomes a fundamental part of her citizens. This can happen only when we accept enterprise as a core nation-building value. This spirit can be easily identified in the history of great industrialized nations.

I wish to point out that enterprise is not primarily about making profit, but rather, it is about pursuing a vision or passion. According to Nick Walters, "Enterprise to me is simply seeing a need and filling it. It doesn't matter whether it is a business or charity. It takes a certain confidence because you are doing something that hasn't been done before, but it is not really that complicated. Whether it is new activity, a new company, or an improvement in something that exists, if you believe in yourself you take it upon yourself to get it done. You believe first, then you get others to believe"

In the words of Arnold W. Craft, "America grew great from the seed of the will to do and dare, the will to get up and go on and not quit after we had erred and fallen: the will to struggle to our feet and plod along and not give up and lie down when we wavered and stumbled from fatigue" Truly, America is a great example of a nation built on the spirit of enterprise. Half of the world 20 largest corporations are based there. Also, a significant number of her citizens are small and medium business owners, not to mention that America has the largest number of charity organizations effecting change in every continent on the globe. This spirit of enterprise is reflected in all areas of the American life, including social works and even politics, and not limited to commerce. It is one of the key factors that enabled an African American aspire to the highest office in the land and achieve that in 2008. President Obama is an excellent example of how the seemingly impossible can be achieved through enterprise.

According to Liberty Hyde Bailey, "There are two essential epochs in any enterprise — to begin, and to get done." From this we can see two key themes in enterprise: initiative and momentum. Enterprise reiterates the fact that building a nation does not lie with the government of that nation alone but mainly with her people. People have to take the initiative to bring positive change in their circle of influence and not just sit down, limited to talking only. Because if we do not take the risk, we will not be able to exploit or create opportunities to fulfil our ambition and effect the change we so greatly desire.

It is the spirit of enterprise founded in our spirituality, the recognition and pursuit of our God given assignment on earth, that will result in the expression of compassion, valour and responsibility; exploitation of opportunities; the pursuit of ambition; and the defence of equality and liberty. While initiative would take the first step of faith into the unknown, it is momentum (persistence) that would sustain the initiative by enabling further steps of faith despite the natural response of fear, uncertainty, disappointment and opposition. Besides faith, other themes in enterprise are innovation, determination, creativity, enthusiasm and competitiveness.

In the pursuit of enterprise, we give our all to that vision we have and the passion we carry. In so doing, we make things better not only for ourselves but also for others in our families, communities and the nation. As important as this core value is to nation-building, like other values, it must be tempered by responsibility, compassion and spirituality to keep its focus on nation-building.

Spirituality

Sometimes people get the mistaken notion that spirituality is a separate department of life, the penthouse of existence. But rightly understood, it is a vital awareness that pervades all realms of our being.
DAVID STEINDL-RAST

Spirituality means the state, quality, manner or fact of being spiritual. By being spiritual we mean believe in God and that we are His creation. Genesis 1:27 says, "So God created man in his own image, in the image of God he created him; male and female he created them." As God is spirit, so are we and we are created in His image, an image that meant dominion over the earth. Spirituality is about our faith in God, His purpose for our nation, His potential sown into us and His enabling to see us exhibit these. It emphasizes the original plan of God for our lives — dominion over the earth as people created equally.

Spirituality, I believe, is the mother of all core values because out of this value comes all the other core values. As American Poet Allen Tate, puts it, "Religion is the sole technique for the validating of values." As a result, the transformation of the thoughts, words and actions through the core values is initiated by this value. Spirituality is primarily about serving God and His people and the true expression of this value will witness Nigerians become transformed from self-focused to nation-focused. This value also provides the freedom and the boundaries within which the other values operate.

The words of former US President, Calvin Coolidge, says it best, "Our doctrine of equality and liberty and humanity comes from our belief in the brotherhood of man through the fatherhood of God. We do not need more national development, we need more spiritual development. We do not need more intellectual power, we need more spiritual power. We do not need more knowledge, we need more character. We do not need more law, we need more religion. We do not need more of things that are seen, we need more of the things that are unseen"

Again, America is great example of a nation with spirituality as a core value. According to Bill Halamandaris, "Whether or not you believe America came from God, it is clear the values that shaped our democracy were founded on religious principles and, in particular, the Christian way of life". It is a well known fact that the Founding Fathers of America were deeply religious and this reflected in the constitution they put together and the apparatus of national identity: Seal, currency, national anthem, and so on. Even till date, the US dollar bill carries the motto – 'In God We Trust' and it is common to hear the statement 'God Bless America' being used by people in government and people outside government. Not to mention the fact that the US Congress still keeps the tradition of opening each session with an opening prayer. Here is a quote by Ronald Reagan, former US President, which highlights the emphasis placed on spirituality by the leadership and people of that country, "I believe with all my heart that standing up for America means standing up for the God who has so blessed our land. We need God's help to guide our nation through stormy seas. But we can't expect Him to protect America in a crisis if we just leave Him over on the shelf in our day-to-day living."

The primary role of this value is the emphasis it places on others rather than on ourselves, starting with the aim to glorify God in all we do for Him and for others (His people). It goes further to state that we, not only our leaders, are accountable to God for what we do with our nation, with the talents, resources and blessings He has endowed us with, individually and as a nation. An excellent example of America's service to God and His people is seen in the fact that America — government and the people — is by far the largest aid donor to third world countries or any disaster stricken region. They also have the highest number of charity organizations and volunteers for charity missions at home and abroad.

According to USA Today in their 25th June 2007 issue, America set a record in charity giving. Below is an excerpt from the report:

Americans gave nearly $300 billion to charitable causes last year, setting a record and besting the 2005 total that had been boosted by a surge in aid to victims of hurricanes Katrina, Rita and Wilma and the Asian tsunami. Donors contributed an estimated $295.02 billion in 2006, a 1% increase when adjusted for inflation, up from $283.05 billion in 2005. Excluding donations for disaster relief, the total rose 3.2%, inflation-adjusted, according to an annual report released Monday by the Giving USA Foundation at Indiana University's Center on Philanthropy.

What people find especially interesting about this, and it's true year after year, that such a high percentage comes from individual donors," Giving USA Chairman Richard Jolly said, individuals gave a combined 75.6% of the total. With bequests, that rises to 83.4%. "It tells you something about American culture that is unlike any other country," said Claire Guadiana, a professor at NYU's Hayman Center for Philanthropy and author of *The Greater Good: How Philanthropy Drives the American Economy and Can Save Capitalism.* Guadiana said the willingness of Americans to give cuts across income levels, and their

investments go to developing ideas, inventions and
people to the benefit of the overall economy."

This expression of generosity by Americans is strong indicator
of her spirituality, no wonder she is nicknamed 'God's Own
Country'. Our appreciation of the role of spirituality is
evident in our national pledge where we call on God to help
us keep our pledge "So help me God" and in the second stanza
of our national anthem where we again call on God to direct
us, our leaders and youths. However, Nigerians are yet to fully
go beyond symbols of spirituality, which includes our passion
for regular attendance of churches and mosques meetings, to
a lifestyle of spirituality.

As Bill Shore, the founder of one of America's largest
private, non-profit organisation, Share Our Strength, puts
it, "The fundamental idea for Share our Strength — that
everybody has a strength to share is very spiritual. Everybody's
been given a gift of some type, and if we can tap into that, if
we can create vehicles in which people can contribute whatever
their particular unique talent or gift is, then that can really
change the world." He further added, "I have come to believe
that being in touch with yourself and what gifts you were given,
trying to understand and nurture them, is a very spiritual
experience. A state of grace exists when who you are to the
world is who you really are inside. Being in touch with your
strengths and your gifts gets you pretty close to that." The next
chapter on how to implement nation-building will focus
more on identifying and putting those God given strengths
and gifts to use.

In conclusion, I quote Bill Halamandaris, "Values are not
hereditary. Great ideals do not live in the hearts and minds of
men simple because they are right. They must be taught. They
must be learned and lived". This, every Nigerian should
commit to do. When we practice the core values, we
strengthen our understanding of these values, especially when
we begin to see the benefit in our lives and that of others. The
initial stage may be challenging but constant and deliberate

efforts will see us convert these values into habits — way of life — keeping in mind why we are building our nation.

How to implement
Nation-Building

Having discussed what we mean by nation-building, why we must build our nation and the core values required to transform our thoughts, we are now prepared to discuss how nation-building is implemented. Oscar Wilde said, "Discontent is the first step in the progress of a man or a nation" We can relate to this, in view of the deep sense of discontentment amongst Nigerians. However, the level of our implementation of nation-building will be determined by the depth of our understanding of what nation-building is and our acceptance of why we must build our nation both of which will impact on how far the core values will transformed our mindset (thoughts).

If we fully commit ourselves to nation-building, we will gain the wisdom, understanding and motivation to implement the right steps with courage, sacrifice, patience and consistency; remembering the words of Friedrich Nietzsche, "He who has a why can endure any how".

The process of implementing nation-building is broken into four sections — *Study, Practice, Teach* and *Inspire*. First, we study to become equipped to practice, then practice to become equipped to teach others and finally, inspire others by our practice and teaching. This is the basic developmental process for any individual and since individuals form a nation, it does provide the process for building a nation. The process applies to all ages and classes of Nigerians. For example, a child or an adult studies by what he or she hears, sees and reads; then puts to practice what has been learnt; goes on to teach people in his or her circle of influence; and ultimately inspires people through consistency in practice and teaching.

The development of the nation depends primarily on the development of her citizens because how every individual lives their life determines the success or failure of that nation. Nigeria will only be what we Nigerians are. This reiterates why nation-building is about our thoughts, words and actions. The famous Chinese teacher, Confucius, said, "To put the world in order, we must first put the nation in order; to put the nation in order, we must put the family in order; to put the family in order, we must cultivate our personal life; and to cultivate our personal life, we must first set our hearts right."

Study

Study the situation thoroughly, go over in your imagination the various courses of action possible to you and the consequences which can and may follow from each course. Pick out the course which gives the most promise and go ahead.
    MAXWELL MALTZ

Study is the very first step in the development of an individual and it is also the first step in implementing nation-building. By study we simply mean to think deeply, reflect or examine closely. Epictetus, the Greek philosopher said "When you are offended at any man's fault, turn to yourself and study your own failings. Then you will forget your anger." Just maybe, we will be less angry with our leaders when we study our own failings and realize we are really not different from them and equally responsible for our failure as a nation.

So, we need to invest the time and resources to think deeply, reflect or examine closely the state of our nation, putting the focus on ourselves because the only way we can change the circumstances surrounding us is by changing what we think, say and do about it. This can only happen when we invest time to study our values, thoughts, words and actions. It requires quiet moments spent in solitude which will help us understand the root cause of our problem, why we need to build, what needs to change in our mindset and how we can use what we have to effect change.

So essential is study that no one has ever reached the pinnacle of any human endeavour without adequate study as a form of preparation. Therefore, if we want to take our nation to the pinnacle of her potential, our study of what nation-building is, why it is needed and how to implement it is mandatory and must come first.

The 4 key steps involved in the study of nation-building are Responsibility, Review, Identification and Planning.

Responsibility

Change will not come if we wait for some other person or some other time. We are the ones we've been waiting for. We are the change that we seek.
PRESIDENT BARACK OBAMA

What you are not responsible for, you do not own. We own this nation Nigeria and we all are responsible for her. This step involves coming to terms with the fact that our nation has not been built, by accepting responsibility for its underdevelopment. We accept responsibility because we note that our beliefs, values, thoughts, words and actions have contributed to the current state of the nation.

If we refused to accept responsibility, we have not accepted the fact that our individual actions lead to the success or failure of the nation. This refusal will block our ability to examine closely and think deeply about our present state of affairs and identify what will be required of us.

To effectively study how we can implement nation-building, we need to have a deep sense of accountability for happenings in our lives and in our nation. It has to be said again, the success or failure of a nation depends on each individual and not just the government.

As a people, we must cease attributing our problems to our leaders or 'they', as we fondly call it, and accept responsibility for whatever happens in our nation. In any case, the nation does belong to us and not just our leaders. This is why responsibility is a core value and the absence of it, is a primary reason why our nation is not yet developed.

To properly study how we can implement nation-building, we must first accept responsibility. This is fundamental and worth reiterating. As stated in the last chapter, responsibility is the fuel that propels thoughts into action. It is the acceptance of responsibility for the current state of our nation that would enable a proper review, identification and planning. Responsibility is the first step as it determines how effective our study of nation-building will be.

Review

Review your work. You will find, if you are honest, that 90% of the trouble is traceable to loafing.

FORD FRICK

Following the acceptance of responsibility for our nation as part of study, we need to review the reasons why we must build our nation and what values we must hold to enable us achieve this goal. By review, we mean to examine critically and deliberately. At this stage we will determine our purpose and motives by resetting our values. This step is essential because accepting responsibility alone will not compel us to identify what role we can play on a general and specific level. Yes, responsibility places a demand on each of us to become responsible for the nation but review will enable us ask the right questions about why we need to become responsible and why we need to change our values.

Since, we have accepted that the onus to build nation is ours, review, then, focuses our minds on why we must build and the values we must be equipped with; thus, giving us the purpose for building and the motivation to undertake the enormous work required. As we stated in the second chapter, *Why nation-building,* we have to address the why before we address the how because "He who has a **why** can endure any how".

Here is a recap of the reasons for building our nation:

We are the nation builders

Don't build, don't inhabit

Best Guarantee for Our Children

Legacy

Sense of fulfilment

Answer the call

Taking back our nation

Establish our dignity

These primary reasons have to be reviewed daily to ensure we are focused on achieving them. As Les Brown puts it, "Review your goals twice every day in order to be focused on achieving them." But to be motivated to daily review the reasons why we must build our nation, our belief system needs to be changed. This is why our core values are essential and must be embedded into the way we think, speak and act. They should also be reviewed daily to enable us grow in our practice and understanding of them.

Compassion

Opportunity

Responsibility

Equality

Valour

Ambition

Liberty
Unity
Enterprise
Spirituality

Review comes before identification because it is in the reviewing of why we must build our nation and change our value system that the process of identifying what we have to offer commences. That is why review is an essential part of the study of how we can implement nation-building and provides an excellent platform for us to identify what we need to change within and what we can change around us. It goes even further than study stage and impacts on the practice stage of nation-building because it provides the fuel that will ensure consistency.

Identification

The place God calls you to is the place where your deep gladness and the world's deep hunger meet.
FREDERICK BUECHNER

After we have accepted responsibility for the current state of our nation and reviewed why it must be built, and changed our values. We are ready to identify what we have to offer by identifying the specific gift, skill, talent, experience and resources inherent in us to effect change. As what we love, learn and want to be remembered for differ, so would what we identify around us. We cannot commit to everything, so to identify our specific area we will need to ask ourselves these questions: What am I good at? What do I love doing? What needs can I serve? What is life asking of me? What gives my life meaning and purpose? What do I feel like I should be doing? In short, what is my conscience directing me to do?

I would like to rely on the views of leadership expert, Stephen Covey, on how to identify what you can do by quoting from his article on *"The 4 Steps to Finding Your Voice"*

Step 1: Tapping into Your Talent: Tapping into your talents starts with understanding where you excel. It involves recognizing your strengths and positioning yourself to leverage them. To tap into your talent consider the question: What am I good at doing?

Step 2: Fuelling Your Passion: When you take part in activities that fill you with positive emotion, you are fuelling your passion. Pursuits that spark your passion bring excitement, enthusiasm, joy, and fun. To fuel your passion, ask yourself: What do I love doing?

Step 3: Being Burdened with a Need: When a problem in society lodges itself in your heart and won't let go, then you have been burdened with a need. Perhaps, the need is an injustice you wish to remedy. Maybe it's a disease you would love to cure. Whatever the case, a burden gnaws at your conscience. To take stock of your biggest burden, wrestle with the question: What need must I serve?

Step 4: Meeting the Need: Once a need has arrested your attention, then you can find your voice by taking action. A need compels you to do something besides criticize from the sidelines. To meet the need, think about this question: How can I align my talent with my passion in order to meet the need that burdens me?

Our nation depends on each of our specific and unique talents to achieve development and the range of skill, talent and passion inherent in us Nigerians, it must be noted, is unlimited. Nothing positively identified should be ignored but rather encouraged.

He who fails to plan, plans to fail.
UNKNOWN

After accepting responsibility, undertaken review and identified areas where we can participate, it is important to plan the line of action to be taken. Planning is so important because the measure of the success achieved in the practice of nation-building will depend to a large extent on the level of planning. I would also add that a proper acceptance of responsibility, an honest review and good identification will affect the quality of our planning.

Whether we have identified a big project or a small effort, there is still some planning required to ensure effectiveness and consistency. Leadership expert, John Maxwell, said, "Planning bridges the gap between our desires and dreams by calling us to action. A concrete plan supplies us with tangible steps to take in the direction of our dreams." I agree with the saying, "He who fails to plan, plans to fail." When we ignore planning we handicap ourselves and stifle the effectiveness of practice. But planning is a relatively simple discipline which everyone can and should do. It requires a window of uninterrupted time for focused thought and jotting down a line of action. It is through planning that we develop a line of action for the practice of nation-building and it helps us prioritise the investment of our resources – money and time.

As we plan let us remember the words of William Danforth, "No plan is worth the paper it is printed on unless it starts you doing something."

Practise

Knowledge is of no value unless you put it into practice.
HEBER J. GRANT

Practice is the natural progression in 'how to implement

nation-building' as we move from study or preparation we proceed to practice — from thoughts to actions and words.

Practice is the act of rehearsing a behaviour over and over or engaging in an activity again and again. It also means translating an idea into action, repetition of an activity to improve skill. It is essential that our practice starts with ourselves and not others. As John Maxwell puts it, "By starting with yourself, you build the self-confidence needed to attract and inspire others."

In practice, our focus is on how we can exercise those thoughts, words and line of actions, developed during the study phase, to build our nation on daily basis. This should be applied generally and specifically as there are areas of practice that we must all participate in and there are areas peculiar to our calling and gift.

There are two key elements in Practice: Initiative and Momentum. We start an action by taking initiative and we persist by keeping the momentum. We will discuss how we practice nation-building under these headings:

Initiative

Success comes from taking the initiative and following up … persisting … eloquently expressing the depth of your love. What simple action could you take today to produce a new momentum toward success in your life?
ANTHONY ROBBINS

To put nation-building into practice, we must steer nation-focused thoughts into words and action, by taking initiative. Initiative is the power or ability to begin or to, energetically, follow through with a plan or task. It is the beginning or introductory step, or opening move — the first of a series of actions.

In our study of how we can implement nation-building, we would have accepted responsibility, reviewed why we need to build and the values to hold, identified what we can do and drawn up a plan. To practice, we now implement our plan by taking initiative. This means, we do not wait for someone or government's approval or permission to practice nation-building, nor do we wait for conditions to be perfect to initiate an action. As stated by Elbert Hubbard, "Initiative is doing the right things without being told."

Taking initiative means that we see what has to be done (the opportunity) and then take the personal responsibility to make it happen. Initiative does not allow circumstance or environment to get in the way and does not make excuses for inability to commence a task. Initiative confronts life's numerous obstacles with a solution-focused attitude, based on the various core nation-building values, instead of a problem-focused attitude. Therefore, initiative is primarily concerned with taking action and that is either starting some new activity or participating in an established activity.

Pioneering Initiative

This refers to making the opening move, leading the way, in an activity. It does not necessarily mean doing something never done before but starting the action to address a specific issue or harness an opportunity. It could be a business, research, invention, social work, advocacy group, political movement, etc.

With the diverse talents, skills and experiences Nigerians have, there is no limit to the amount of initiatives we can pioneer. Thus the core values are essential because the spirit of these values will enable more people to launch out of their comfort zone and pioneer initiatives that will build our nation.

Participating Initiative

This refers to participation in an existing activity. It could be general activities like paying taxes, punctuality, observing traffic rules, carrying out civil duties, e.g., participation in the electoral process, dedicating time and resources to participate in an existing enterprise, movement, charity that enables the building of the nation. Sometimes less challenging than pioneering initiative but it still shares the need to begin an activity. It must be noted that all Nigerians should engage in both pioneering and participating initiatives.

Bill Halamandaris stated, "While all wastage is an affront to God, the greatest waste is the waste of time and the waste of potential" I believe, potential is not really for the benefit of an individual but for their family, community and nation. By taking initiative, we go beyond our comfort zone and it is only then that we significantly learn, change, grow and maximise our potential. The result is our families, community and nation reaps the benefits, while we gain the ultimate reward: a deep sense of fulfilment.

Momentum

She acquires momentum as she advances.
VIRGIL

The English dictionary defines momentum as the impetus to go forward, develop, or get stronger. It is also the strength or force that keeps growing. Any moving body or object possesses momentum and if stationary, it has no momentum (stagnation). Momentum means motion or movement.

In the practice of nation-building, initiative is concerned with taking the first step, making the opening move, but momentum is concerned with sustaining that step or move and giving it more pace and scope. Leadership expert, John Maxwell, explains it this way, "A train travelling 55 mph on a railroad track can crash through a 5-foot thick steel-reinforced concrete wall without stopping. That same train, starting from a stationary position, won't be able to go through an inch-thick block in front of the driving wheel." It is never the size of your problem that is the problem. It's a lack of momentum. Without momentum, even a tiny obstacle can prevent you from moving forward. With momentum, you'll navigate through problems and barely even notice them.

The train of change that will sweep across our nation bringing with it the building of our nation will start with the initiatives brought about by the transformation of thoughts through change in values. But it would only be sustained by the momentum of its motion, breaking down all obstacles and getting us to our destination.

The power of momentum produces people who see less of problems but more possibilities. These are positive people who believe that there is nothing they cannot achieve as the momentum given to their initiatives gives them more understanding, valour and faith to conquer all obstacles. Under study, we accepted responsibility, reviewed the situation and what we required and we identified what we could offer, with a plan of action. It is initiative that moves that plan from the drawing board into action and it is momentum that creates the daily habits that ensures consistency in action, avoids stagnation and produces excellence. According to Aristotle, "We are what we repeatedly do. Excellence, then, is not an act, but a habit." These are the transformation momentum produces in our lives (a new lifestyle focused on building the nation). According to leadership expert, Jim Rohn, "Whatever good things we build end up building us."

The other transformation produced by momentum is the shifting of focus from the past to the present and future. As a nation, we have focused too long on our past and as a result, have not focused enough on our present and future to put to practice the lessons learnt. As stated by John Maxwell, "Many people have powerful dreams. However, most don't realize that the viability of their ideal tomorrow is based on what they do today. The difference between a dream and wishful thinking is what you're doing now. Practice today what you want to be tomorrow. If you do it well enough, someday you may arrive at your dream."

When we develop momentum in our practice of nation-building, it inputs into us creativity, positive attitude and habits, discipline, teamwork — causes us to share our vision with other Nigerians and incorporate their participation — fuels passion, builds character, introduces changes in us and then around us, inputs into us a sense of gratitude for what we have and the opportunity and valour to take more initiatives. Our practice will witness significant courage, focus, consistency, and more importantly, greater pace and scope. At this point, the nation-building train has not just departed but is now gathering speed.

It is okay to have a big vision developed in the study phase but for effective initiative and momentum, it is essential to break the big vision into small manageable and achievable goals. When goals are small and viable, they are within immediate reach and the attainment of these small goals all add up into a big change. Not to mention the fact that people will be won over as they see the progress being made. One of the greatest college basketball coaches of all time, John Wooden, said, "When you improve a little each day, eventually big things occur ... Don't look for the quick, big improvement. Seek the small improvement one day at a time. That's the only way it happens and when it happens, it lasts."

Teach

Any genuine teaching will result, if successful, in someone knowing how to bring about a better condition of things than existed earlier.
JOHN DEWEY

The key dictionary definitions for Teaching are: to impart knowledge or skill; to advocate or preach; to give instruction; to cause to learn by example or experience. I would add that Teaching is also an expression of optimism as stated by Colleen Wilcox, "Teaching is the greatest act of optimism".

It is not enough for us to identify what we can and will do to build our nation and to put them into practice. Mass participation is required in nation-building (we can not do it on our own) and that is why it is essential to undertake nation-focused thoughts, words and actions with a view to not only building our nation but to teach others to do likewise.

It is even when we are teaching others that we gain further insights and understanding into what we are practicing. Teaching serves both the student and the teacher. Tryon Edwards said, "If you would thoroughly know anything, teach it to others." Also Aristotle commented that, "Teaching is the highest form of understanding." There is a saying that "Teachers teach more by what they are than by what they say". Therefore, it is important to note that we will make limited impact if we do not practice what we teach. After all, it is commonly stated that experience is the best teacher. The experience gained from practicing nation-building places us in an excellent position by equipping us to teach others. But also, it takes our teaching from the theoretical to the practical, providing real life case studies of what can and has been achieved. Teaching also affords us the opportunity to enable others avoid the mistakes we made which would help accelerate the process for those we teach.

People learn mainly by observing than by hearing. This is why in the steps on how to implement nation-building Teaching comes after Practice. The momentum we carry in our practice of nation-building will naturally provide for us a platform to teach through words and deeds. A famous saying goes, "Practice what you preach" and I believe it is worth adding, 'and teach what you practice'. We have to teach what we practice in all areas of influence: at home, business or workplace and in our community with the objective of producing nation-builders — people who would also study, practice, teach and inspire nation-building.

There are 3 elements in teaching: to tell (Communication), to show (Model) and to involve (Mentor). To become effective in teaching nation-building, we must teach daily by communicating, modelling and mentoring.

Communication

Words are, of course, the most powerful drug used by mankind.
RUDYARD KIPLING

Communication is the common form of teaching and by communication we mean the act of communicating or the imparting of thoughts, opinions or information by speech or writing. Effective communication is not just what we communicate, it is also the ability to listen, understand and appreciate the position of the other party. It also involves non-verbal forms like gestures and position. To teach nation-building via effective communication, we have to see our home, work or business place, marketplace and community, in fact everywhere we come in contact with people, as our classroom.

Below are some points, to note for effective communication, adapted from the book *Interpersonal Communication: Relating to Others* by Steven Beebe, Susan Beebe and Mark Redmond. Interspersed with my explanation:

Focus on what you know with passion: Regularly communicate your own desires and vision rather than evaluating others. Instead of making assumptions about other people or situations, our focus should be on information, observations and specific issues like what is nation-building, why we need to build, nation-building values and how we are building the nation

Focus on the issue, not the person: This one, Nigerians need to learn. We should endeavour not to take everything personal and to ensure this, our focus should be on the issue — building a great nation and not on individuals, past or present leaders or ordinary Nigerians,

Focus on people understanding our communications rather than on what we are communicating: After all, effective communication is about the listener.

Be genuine and not manipulative: Be yourself, honest and open. Be consistent in what you communicate and no better way of achieving this except you practice what you teach. This shows integrity to yourself and people around you.

Empathize rather than remain detached: Communicate from the platform of relationship and compassion. This requires sensitivity to where they are and what they are going through. When we communicate on this basis, we gain trust and those who trust us, listen to what we have to say.

Be flexible towards others: Another key point for Nigerians. Allow people to share their point of view even if we don't agree because flexibility requires us to respect different views. Arguments serve no purpose in communication.

Value yourself and your own experiences: Passion is not enough in effective communication, deep conviction is required. This is borne out of the core nation-building values we hold and the experiences we have had. Such conviction consciously and unconsciously expresses itself in our communication.

Present yourself as an equal rather than a superior: We must ensure we come around as equals to the people we communicate with, to enable us get their attention and for them to understand our messages. All Nigerians are equals and have equal share in the nation, so must see others, educated or uneducated, as equal co-builders.

Use confirming responses: We have to response verbally and non-verbally to people in ways that acknowledges their experiences. We ask questions, receive response, provide positive feedback by thanking them for their input, confirming their rights to hold such opinion even when we disagree, and provide our view.

Be consistent between verbal and no-verbal cues: Non-verbal cues are said to be more convincing than verbal messages. Therefore, alongside consistent positive verbal communication, we have to exhibit positive non-verbal communication consistently as well. We communicate more effectively when we give attention to our verbal and non-verbal cues.

Model

Fortunately, most human behaviour is learned observationally through modelling: from observing others one forms an idea of how new behaviours are performed, and on later occasions this coded information serves as a guide for action.

ALBERT BANDURA

Model means a standard or example for imitation or comparison. While the first element in teaching has to do with what we say and how we say it, this second element in teaching nation-building is focused on what we do that becomes an example or a model. Though our method of communication can be a model, the key emphasis here is on how we live our lives.

Because it is focused on our lifestyle, it is the most important element in teaching, in this case, teaching nation-building. According to Albert Einstein, "Setting an example is not the main means of influencing another, it is the only means." We have to remember that what we practice is what we model consciously and unconsciously. Therefore, there is little impact when we communicate nation-building and our lifestyle shows that we are self-focused and not nation-focused. This contradiction leads to loss of integrity, respect and attention. Inevitably, people will ignore what we say and replicate what we model because modelling is more powerful than the talking we do (we sure do a lot of talking). It is claimed that most people learn more by what they see than by what they hear.

This element highlights why the problem with Nigeria does not rest with our political leaders but on every Nigerian. The model we copy is that of our parents, brothers, sisters, neighbours, teachers, church or mosque members and every person in our circle of daily interaction. Whether we accept it or not, we are all role models (positive or negative). Our nation is where it is today because of the sort of models we have in abundance. To teach nation-building we have to show a different way or approach to doing things.

Effective modelling requires that we all have models we consistently learn from and we model what we have learnt. This can be achieved by proactively deciding the sort of friendship we keep and gaining inspiration through reading biographies of present and past models. The famous Greek philosopher, Epictetus, recommended, "Imagine for yourself a character, a model personality, whose example you determine to follow, in private as well as in public." The famous American civil rights activist, Rosa Park, best summed it up, "Each person must live their life as a model for others." This should be the motto of every nation-builder — living their life as a model for others.

I believe, an effective model is someone who firmly believes in and daily expresses the core values we discussed in chapter two.

Compassion: Model a lifestyle of compassion to family, friends and strangers

Opportunity: Seek for themselves and offer to others, the opportunity to advance life's legitimate goals and aspiration

Responsibility: Responsible in thoughts, words and actions internally and to the family, community and nation.

Equality: Demand equality for themselves and for others.

Valour: Exhibits a lifestyle of courage in private and in public circles.

Ambition: Ambitious to do great things for the nation

Liberty: Defend their liberties and that of others

Unity: Promotes unity in thoughts, words and actions at all times

Enterprise: Propagate and pursue their dreams with long term commitment

Spirituality: Model a lifestyle that is deeply rooted in faith in God and His purpose for their lives.

Any model that lives these values is bound to reproduce many others who will be inspired to go on and do same. In so doing, nation-building is taught in deeds and not just words.

Mentor

A message prepared in the mind reaches a mind; a message prepared in a life reaches a life.

BILL GOTHARD

Mentor means a wise and trusted counsellor, guide or advisor. A mentor has been through the exact thing you are going through on your journey and as a result, their hindsight can become your foresight. It is mainly considered an exclusive type of teaching meant for those with a wealth of experience, who may sit in a position of influence. A mentor is usually an older individual who helps and guides the development of others without personal gain.

Mentoring is also concerned with creating an informal environment in which one person can feel encouraged to discuss their needs and circumstances openly and in confidence with another person who is in a position to be of help to them.

Mentoring is a combination of communicating and modelling, with emphasis on regular contact. Rather than a general approach, its strategy is to focus on a target group or person. As a result, mentoring produces significant results as a form of teaching.

It is important for positive models to naturally progress to become mentors. This is because as models, people are drawn to them out of admiration for and attraction to their lifestyle and those drawn would consider the models their mentors. However, to become a mentor requires a decision and a commitment because it would place a demand on your time that will be invested in those being mentored.

If modelling achieves so much in teaching nation-building, mentoring sustains and structures such gains. While modelling will produce people who will commence the process of change, mentoring takes it one step further. It calls for vision, goals, accountability and focus that will bring about those desired changes and ensure its sustenance in the long term.

A mentor is a guide and not only school children need guides. All age groups need a guide and as with modelling, we should make a commitment to come under a guide and also be a guide.

A nation-focused mentor guides the mentored through the study phase: responsibility, review, identification and planning; the practice phase: initiatives and momentum; and the teaching phase of nation-building. Mentoring could be in any area of development — personal development, health, education, technology, charity work, child welfare, faith, career, business, community, politics, commerce, sports, etc. It is the ultimate level of teaching for every nation-builder. We should all seek to mentor others on how we can build a great nation, in our specific area of influence. We all need mentors most especially the youths.

No nation can make progress without the passing over of the confidence, knowledge and resources from the older to the younger generation. We need to create an environment of relationships, people bonding with people with the purpose of assisting them to be all they can and should be.

Key roles of a mentor as advocated by the Coaching and Mentoring Network

- Facilitates the exploration of needs, motivations, desires, skills and thought processes to assist the mentee (the person being mentored) in making real, lasting change.
- Uses questioning techniques to facilitate mentee's own thought processes in order to identify solutions and actions rather than taking a wholly directive approach
- Supports the mentee in setting appropriate goals and methods of assessing progress in relation to these goals.
- Encourages a commitment to action and the development of lasting personal growth and change.
- Observes, listens and ask questions to understand the mentee's situation. Maintains unconditional positive regard for the mentee, which means that the mentor is at all times supportive and non-judgmental of the mentee's views, lifestyle and aspirations.
- Creatively apply tools and techniques which may include one-on-one training, facilitating counselling and networking.
- Ensures that mentee develops personal competence and does not develop an unhealthy dependence on the mentoring relationship.
- Evaluates the outcomes of the process, using objective measures wherever possible to ensure the relationship is successful and the mentee is achieving their personal goals.
- Encourages mentee to continually improve competencies and to develop new developmental alliances where necessary to achieve their goals.
- Work within their area of personal competence.
- Possesses qualifications and experience in the areas that skills-transfer mentoring is offered.
- Manages the relationship to ensure the mentee receives the appropriate level of service and that programmes are neither too short nor too long.

Culled from The Coaching and Mentoring Network website

From the above listed key roles of a mentor, it is obvious that the human capital development which is a prerequisite for nation-building is effectively addressed by mentoring. There is no greater contribution to humanity than investing in others our experience, skill, expertise, passion and dreams.

Inspire

The mediocre teacher tells. The good teacher explains. The superior teacher demonstrates. The great teacher inspires.
WILLIAM ARTHUR WARD

The English dictionary defines Inspiration as the means to simulate to action, energies and ideals. To produce or arouse a feeling, thought, etc. To influence or impel, to prompt or instigate utterances, acts, etc., by influence. To give rise to, bring about, cause, etc.

The ultimate in the implementation of nation-building is to inspire. Because it is the final destination for a person who has studied, practiced and taught nation-building generally and specifically. The same truth applies to every area of human endeavours, but I must add nation-building is central to all endeavours.

A person inspires not just the immediate people or current generation but a wider audience and generations to come by their exceptional thoughts expressed in inspirational words and actions. They inspire through a consistent lifestyle, breaking new grounds or records, defying myths, removing limitations and raising the bar or standard to be attained. The famous American Poet, Ralph Waldo Emerson, said, "In art the hand can never execute anything higher than the heart can inspire". I believe, in life as in art, we can never execute anything higher than our mind can inspire. It is the people who inspire us that enable us break the limitations of our minds. Sometimes we do not need to look any further than within our own circle of family and friends. At other times, we are inspired by those we know only by name.

Nation-builders who inspire are people who have accepted responsibility for their nation, identified specific areas to effect change, with a line of action to initiate and maintain that change, communicated and modelled it to others and mentored others or gained disciples.

When we undertake critical analysis of any nation-builder, we will find someone that inspired them to believe the impossible, to rise up with courage and pursue their dreams with full commitment. This is why inspiration from others is a prerequisite for nation-building but before we can see such people , they must first study, practice and teach nation-building because these are the qualities of people who inspire. If we are honest, we are all attracted to people who inspire. Again, Ralph Emerson said, "Our chief want is someone who will inspire us to be what we know we could be."

The sum total of people who inspire is the legacy they leave for present and future generations. The significant contribution they make becomes a reference point or case study of how the impossible is made possible.

In the last chapter of this book, Case Studies of Nation-Building, we shall discuss the contributions of a few people to nation-building. These are people whose contributions are not limited to what they did but also the inspiration they were to many others, including many of us today.

Summary

It may be obvious already but it has to be emphasized that the implementation of nation-building is putting the core nation-building values to work at every stage of the process. Leadership expert, Stephen B. Covey, said, " ... You must prepare the ground, plant the seed, cultivate and water if you expect to reap the harvest." So, it is the citizens that must prepare the ground – study, plant the seed – practice, cultivate and water – teach and inspire in order for us to reap the harvest of a developed nation. God will not come down from heaven to build the nation for us neither can foreigners do it for us. Nigeria is our house and it is solely ours to build.

chapter five

Foundation for Nation-Building: The Family

There is no doubt that it is around the family and the home that all the greatest virtues, the most dominating virtues of human society, are created, strengthened and maintained

WINSTON CHURCHILL

The three key foundations for nation-building are: the Family, Faith and Education. These foundations are the biggest influencers of change in the people of any nation and no nation can be built without these foundations. We will focus on Family and Faith because Education can be well catered for when nation-building is active in both the Family and Faith.

As important as Faith is, the family comes first and is the main foundation. This is because the family is the primary cell of a nation and the coming together of the various cells forms a community and a nation is a group of communities. Therefore, the family is the most important foundation of the nation and is the main place for the study, practice, teaching and inspiration of nation-building. Anyone that aspires to be a nation-builder must begin with the family. The values practiced within the family will reflect upon the nation.

The famous Chinese philosopher, Confucius, said, "The strength of a nation is derived from the integrity of its homes." It is in the family that real training, leadership by serving and values are taught and practiced. It is on this basis that we must view the role of the family in nation-building as the foundation of development. Therefore, the underdevelopment of our nation is as a result of the poor quality of the family. This supports the view that our political leadership is not the real problem of our nation. The problem and solution is the family. As propounded by Confucius, "To put the world right in order, we must first put the nation in order; to put the nation in order, we must first put the family in order ... "

The family gives us our identity and provides us with moral, social and economic support. Each person in the family has capabilities, abilities and gifts and it is the role of the family in nation-building to facilitate these within limits of the nation-building core values. When this is achieved, the family produces people who are well trained, in values, and are nation focused, which will culminate in a developed nation.

My focus will be on the two main characters in the family — the Father and the Mother — because they play the dominant role in determining and shaping the direction of the family.

Fatherhood

The single biggest social problem in our society may be growing absence of fathers from their children's homes because it contributes to so many social problems ... Without a father to help guide, without a father to care, without a father to teach men to be men, and to teach girls to expect respect from men, it's harder ...

PRESIDENT BILL CLINTON

Children are the main building blocks in building the future of any nation but the older generations are the builders. No group among the older generation has more impact on these 'building blocks' like parents, especially the fathers. Various researches have shown that children who grow with actively involved fathers are less likely to smoke or get into trouble with the police. These children achieve better levels of education, develop good friendships with children of both sexes, have better relationships with their partners and a greater sense of spiritual, mental and physical well-being as adults. These benefits show the importance of fathers to nation-building and also emphasises the fact that the foundation of our children development must be laid by the father.

The most important role in the family is played by the father. To highlight this, we shall look at who the father is, before addressing his role in nation-building. Our understanding of who the father is will explain why the father is required in nation-building.

Leader – The father is the head of the family and is responsible for directing the family.

Image of God - Pope John XXIII said, "Within the family, the father stands in God's place." It means that a father has the task of reflecting the image of God and the result is the child's initial and, in some cases, constant view of God is based on their relationship with their father.

Protector - This role includes physical, emotional, mental, and spiritual protection. As children we particularly need protection, and we need to have our values, purity, and honour protected into adulthood. A father protects his children from physical, spiritual and emotional harm.

Provider - This is perhaps one of the more instinctive roles of a father. A father provides necessities and an environment for growth through love and encouragement. Fathers provide for the children what they may not be able to provide for themselves while teaching them how to eventually become independent.

Enforcer – The father is the family enforcer. He emphasizes the rules and disciplines when they are broken.

Counsellor - A father is a guide and mentor. He directs his children toward the path in life that promises to fit them best.

Role Model – By virtue of this position, a father automatically becomes a role model for his children. This could be positive or negative modelling, either consciously or unconsciously.

Friend - It is said that a child learns how to interact with others on the lap of a father. A healthy friendship with a father gives the children confidence, trust and a good understanding of boundaries, understanding of what is safe and what is not.

The Primary Role of Fathers in Nation-Building

While the wife is the manager of the home, the man is the manager of the wife and by extension of the family. This means, the primary role of father in nation-building is providing leadership in the home. One of the key reasons for the collapse of any society is the absence fathers (both those away from their family home and those present but not involved). For nation-building to occur, fathers need to rise up to their responsibility in providing participatory leadership to their wives and children in both spiritual and physical matters.

Specifically, the primary role of fathers is expressed in two key areas: Teaching and Messaging.

Teaching

It is not possible for one to teach others who cannot teach his own family.
   CONFUCIUS

The main role of fathers in nation-building is in teaching nation-building core values to their family. Here the emphasis is on 'sowing' and 'watering' the 'seeds' required for building the nation. Like we observed in the chapter four, *How to implement nation-building*, teaching comes in the form of communication, modeling and mentoring. The values, again, are Compassion, Opportunity, Responsibility, Equality, Valour, Ambition, Liberty, Unity, Enterprise and Spirituality.

Communication: It is the father's role as family head to ensure that each of the nation-building values is well communicated to every member of the family. By communicate, we mean it has to be clearly written out and displayed where the family can regularly see it; thoroughly explained in the language the children will understand using stories, including personal experiences, to provide examples and illustrations; regular appraisals should be conducted to see how the family is doing in each area; the use of other communication tools, books, relevant movies, television and internet programmes and real life experiences, to further illustrate and emphasis the values; consistency in discipline with appropriate punishment when values are broken and appropriate rewards when they are expressed.

Modelling: For greater result and impact, fathers are to model each of the values to their children in their daily lives. "Example is not the main thing in influencing others. It is the only thing." (Albert Schweizer)

There is no better way to teach than by modelling. For example, we model compassion by giving our time and resources to someone in need in the presence of our family; we model responsibility by not blaming others but taking responsibility for our lives, words, actions and admitting it when we are wrong and apologising; we teach unity by developing strong friendship with our wives, children, neighbours, people from other ethnic groups and different religious background; we teach spirituality by modelling a life of deep devotion and commitment to God in prayer, study of His Word, worship, fellowship with other believers and living an obedient life; we model ambition by emphasizing our vision to our family; and enterprise by pursuing that vision with deep passion and focus; we model equality by treating people around us as equals with dignity and pride, irrespective of class or sex; we model opportunity by providing all our children and people around us the best opportunity to become what they desire to be and by providing them with opportunities to put the nation-building values into regular practice; we model valour by showing courage in volunteering to help in any crisis situation including injustices; finally, we model liberty by providing an environment for people to fully express themselves, including people that serve us, and dedicating resources to fight for the oppressed in our society.

The end product of this would be our family seeing us as positive role models and emulating us. We must remember that our children are watching and listening, even when we don't think they are. There is a famous saying by an unknown author which states that "Every father should remember that one day his son will follow his example instead of his advice".

Parents who don't practice what they preach send a very clear message to their children that it is okay to say one thing and do another. Here lies the foundation for the deceptive lives many live in our nation today.

Mentoring: In addition to modelling, our families require mentors who will guide their development. Fathers are perfectly fitted for this role.

Through modelling, children are taught by the example of how fathers live their lives but through mentoring, fathers work closely with the children. In this case, they teach the nation-building values by implementing each value with them.

For example, to mentor them in the area of compassion, we serve others together. This could be a community development project like distributing foodstuff, clothes, medication to the less privileged. With the child working alongside the father, they receive direct mentoring on how to express compassion and they learn details involved in the act as well e.g., hugging the recipients, sitting down with them, sharing stories, food or drinks with them to make them feel valued.

To mentor them in enterprise, we work with them to go beyond the normal requirements for success by encouraging them to press on beyond the 'pain barrier' with extra efforts to enable them become the best in their pursuit.

To mentor them in spirituality, we encourage their partnership with us in worshiping, praying, studying the word, going to fellowship together. We should never miss an opportunity to let them know that we enjoy their participation in such activities.

We mentor them in ambition by working with them to define their goals, set targets to achieve them, have regular appraisals to evaluate progress and fine tune targets, if required, and introduce new goals when previous ones have been achieved.

We mentor them in responsibility by entrusting important task to them to implement. We will also see the values of opportunity and valour come into operation as they seek to achieve the task we have set for them. Participating in activities like camping, Boys Scout, Girls Guide, and so on. is a key way to implement this.

As part of mentoring, fathers should provide their children with books on Nigerian history and great nation-builders from across the globe and to encourage and model to them, we should read such books too.

Messaging

The destiny of the world is determined less by the battles that are lost and won than by the stories it loves and believes in.
HAROLD GODDARD

The second primary role of fathers is in the area of messaging – stories they tell their children. Stories are an effective way of moulding children which offers the fathers an excellent opportunity to informally educate and inform their children about their country. Many Nigerians have fond memories of the storytelling programme, *Tales by Moonlight*, usually aired on NTA Network Service on Sunday evenings.

According to Robert McKee Brown, "Storytelling is the

most powerful way to put ideas into the world today". The objective here is to give our children the background of our nation's past, its present and the sort of future we desire for her. After all, according to Bill Mooney and David Holt in, *The Storyteller's Guide*, "History is nothing but a series of stories, whether it be world history or family history."

The reason why we tell our children stories is: to help them connect with previous generations of the family and community, appreciating what challenges they faced and how they dealt with it; make them know and feel part of the family history especially when they hear about the contributions of their fathers or ancestors to nation-building; prepare them to handle life's challenges with the knowledge that their father or relative have faced similar challenges and came through, some with failures and some with success; and pass on the vision of their ancestors to enable the children carry on the battles to actualize the family and community's dreams. As the Siberian saying goes, "If you don't know the trees you may be lost in the forest, but if you don't know the stories you may be lost in life."

Also, telling our children stories of our lives is a great privilege and an opportunity to communicate to our children what is in our heart which could contribute to the moral upbringing of our children. The lessons within these stories can provide some of the moral anchor for our kids in a world that does not often provide moral anchors. It is also a means to preserve tradition, values, vision and inspiration, not to mention that our children will most likely repeat this to their children.

It must be noted that this role requires fathers to become more actively involved in their children's development, and the success of our storytelling in the lives of our children will be based on a good father-child relationship.

The key areas to cover in stories are:

Nation-building

Through storytelling fathers can communicate what nation-building is, why it is needed (the benefits), values required and how it is implemented. The stories must include how we model nation-building in our daily activities; how members of our families and community, past and present, modelled nation-building; and how inspirational figures like Gani Fawehinmi, Obafemi Awolowo, Ahmadu Bello, The Kuti Family, Nnamdi Azikiwe and many others, modelled nation-building in Nigeria.

Nigerian History

It is an important for children to be taught the history of their country. This is a key role for fathers and storytelling can easily facilitate this. Fathers can use stories to educate their children on what Nigeria was like before the Europeans came, when they first came and where they landed, what brought them, the slave trade, the amalgamation of northern and southern Nigeria, life under colonial rule, the fight for independence, military coups and their impact, the civil war, state creation when and why, overviews of each administration, military and civilian, etc. The stories should include the positives and the negatives and mention family or community member who played a part in our history.

The Future of Nigeria

Though stories are mainly about the past, it can also provide a vehicle to communicate the dreams we have for the future. As fathers are responsible for the direction of the family, and by extension, the nation, stories can help project how a developed Nigeria will look like and how her people will benefit from that. The result will create in the minds of our children the vision and the inspiration to dedicate their lives to building and sustaining a great nation.

To ensure great success in their nation-building role, father would have to make a firm decision and commitment to minimize self-interest and prioritise the investment of time required to build their wives and children. This will require an enormous sacrifice but this is the primary role of fathers. Our success in any other endeavour is not comparable to our success in building our families and again, by extension building our nation. I would reiterate that the absence of fathers is one of the primary reasons for the underdevelopment of our nation. Therefore, every father should seek to effectively raise their children and also other fatherless children.

So important is fatherhood in the Bible that the Old Testament ends with the prophet Malachi highlighting the role of fathers in the renewal of the faith, the family, and nation: "He will turn the hearts of the fathers to their children, and the hearts of the children to their fathers; or else I will come and strike the land with a curse." (Malachi 4:6). It is upon the men that God has laid the responsibility of leadership, guidance and direction. I do believe men will be held accountable for the outcome of the family and nation.

Motherhood

The house does not rest upon the ground, but upon a woman
MEXICAN PROVERB

According to Benjamin Disraeli, a former British Prime Minster, "You can tell the strength of a nation by the women behind its men." This quote best describes the role of women in nation-building — providing full and valuable support to the efforts of men in building the home. The man is the manager of the woman but the woman is the manager of the home and that means the woman's support is required to achieve nation-building in the home.

Again, the family is the foundation of any society and through the mothers' influence on their children, they, together with fathers, create and preserve the values of the society. Motherhood is the greatest role God has conferred upon women. It is the task of creating and building life. As it is true with all tremendous honours and privileges, immense responsibilities accompanies motherhood. While father and mother are to share in bringing the child into the world and in training their children, the mother exerts a unique influence as no other person.

Before we look at the role of mothers in nation-building, let us determine who a mother is and in the process answer the question of why the mother is required in nation-building.

Gives Birth: Every human being came into this world through a woman, a mother.

Servant of the home: The woman is manager of the home but also her servant. She ensures the needs of the family and the needs of the house are catered for. Not only the needs but problems in the home are dumped on mothers and they graciously and consistently take care of these. They nurture the family through service.

Image of God: They reflect the love of God because the love of a mother is the closest human equivalent of God's love. She may lose her patience, her temper but not her love for her children. Her unconditional love, like God's, seems to have no bounds as she exhibits a consistent flow of sacrifice and forgiveness.

Nurturer: Mothers are flexible, open, sensitive, and adaptable and as a result are a key source of constant strength and affection to their children and husband. They provide a listening ear for concerns and fears to be shared without judging and so, are normally confided in. Mothers have the ability to sense when their child or husband is troubled both in their presence or absence.

Role Model: Mothers model the life of service, diligence and hardwork to their family through daily acts of service.

Teacher: They are the first teachers of children. Mothers teach children how to sit, crawl, walk, eat, dress, etc. They also teach the children how to treat people, conduct themselves and serve others.

The primary roles of Mothers in nation-building

I believe the primary roles of mothers in nation-building are responsibility and investment of time. It is in these key areas that mothers support fathers in their leadership role and make the home an excellent platform to build and sustain the nation.

Responsibility

Because mothers are primarily responsible for nurturing the child and managing the home, the responsibility for using the home as a foundation for nation-building must be accepted by mothers. Everything else rest upon accepting this. Though fathers are ultimately held accountable for the home, mothers have great influence over the decisions fathers make and their implementation, so mothers are extremely important to the outcome of the home. In fact, mothers have a greater influence on the character of children due to the fact that, in most cases, the children see the mother more. It is therefore pertinent for mothers to be involved in nation-building using their home as a platform.

In the third chapter that focused on core nation-building values, we stated that the responsibility for building the nation rested with the citizens and not on Aso Rock and various government arms. After all, they are all products of a family and the family is the primary cell of the nation. As managers of the family, mothers hold the key to ensuring the effective implementation of nation-building.

This might seem like preaching to the converted because in most homes, the mother is responsible for the home but seeing the home as a nation-building platform is looking at things slightly differently. It is:
  - managing the home with a purpose - viewing each activity in the home as an opportunity to build our nation.
  - training the children to become nation-focused rather than

self-focused.
- creating in the child the vision to use their God given gifts, abilities, skills and experience for the benefit of the nation.
- modelling a lifestyle of service to others for the benefit of the nation.

In summary, it is about instilling the nation-building values into the child and providing full support to the Father's messaging and teaching.

When mothers accept responsibility for nation-building, they do not view their motherly roles as a duty but as a gift and tool to accomplish the objective of creating a better society for the coming generations. It is a privilege for mothers to be the nurturer of nation-builders and by accepting responsibility, they will be able to support the fathers in identifying what the family can and should do to contribute to the nation, how it will be done, what role each person is to play and the commitment, time and resources, required.

It is now obvious that the success of the fathers in implementing nation-building in the home is dependent on the support given by the mothers. However, I must reiterate that the level of support from mothers is determined by how much responsibility is accepted. It is worth noting that there will be cases where it would be the mother who initiates nation-building efforts in the family and the father will eventually get involved when he sees the benefits and impact of such efforts.

Investment of Time

Again, it might seem quite obvious because motherhood take up a lot of time. But another primary role of mothers in nation-building is a purposeful and consistent commitment to sufficient amount of time required to manage a home focused on nation-building. Because nation-building effort is essentially about serving others, the time required for such commitment is huge but the benefits are rewarding for the family and the nation. Besides the investment of time in the traditional roles of nurturing the family and instilling the nation-building values, time is also required to be invested in supporting other families in the community, especially underprivileged children who are always a concern of mothers.

Unfortunately, our society is following the footsteps of developed nations where an increasing number of mothers have fulltime careers but as ours is an underdeveloped society with little or no laws that provides the support mothers need to combine the roles of homemaker and income earner, the result is that our society is seeing an increasing number of homes where the children are not receiving sufficient care nor learning life skills from mothers as they really should be. It is the nation that gets poorer for it, with Nigerians reaping the 'poor harvest' as can be seen in the poor attitude of our youths and the various social crimes committed by them.

To develop the nation, it is pertinent that most mothers have to make the sacrifice of staying at home to invest the time required to build the nation through their homes. I said, most mothers because there are a few exceptions where the mother is the sole parents or the sole breadwinner. It is the life skills mothers invest in their children that would provide them with practical skills to use in serving their own family and the nation. This includes cooking, homemaking art, learning how to crochet, sewing and knitting, home decorating and organizing, refinishing furniture, bargain shopping, house cleaning, the art of hospitality, living within your means, various forms of handiwork and the list goes on.

Education is essential for the development of our nation and our education system focuses a lot on teaching academic subjects. This teaching is not enough because they do not teach life skills like communication, conflict resolution, parenting, family dynamics, critical thinking, home economics and values. This is why the role of mothers in imparting life skills to their families is essential as it complements the academic training and in the end, transforms our children into nation-builders. Obviously, building a strong home is not a part time role and is not one to be left to the dictates of child minders, house helps and schools. Moreover, we must remember nation-building demands that time is also given to the care, nurture and training of those children outside our families.

The investment of time is required to ensure the proper planning of children routine, regularly assessing their academic progress, encouraging extra-curriculum activities that will build their character, daily imparting of nation-building values through messaging and modelling, training in etiquettes, enforcing discipline, supporting father's nation-building efforts, being readily available to advise, support, encourage and impart the vision of creating a better nation, supporting less privileged mothers and their children, and so on.

It is important for mothers to accept responsibility for their homes. However, it will require the sacrifice of careers to pursue the goal of developing the nation through the family. The investment of time is of greater value than money, producing long term gains. I believe, this role is fundamental to the success of nation-building. According to James W. Boyd, "What we sow, we reap. That is true in every realm, and in no realm is it more evident than in the family unit and development in which the mother is a major component. Many mothers sow in tears, work, self-denial, pain and sacrifice but they will reap in joy and find their highest happiness when they can see the purity, nobility, goodness and Christ likeness in the lives of their children."

For us to not only build a great nation but to also preserve what we have built for many generations to come, we have to promote and defend the role of fulltime mothers committed to using their homes as a platform to build the nation. It is possible for mothers to love their children but not motherhood (in fact, the trend is on the increase). But it is important for mothers to love and value motherhood as much as they love their children. That is what the investment of time and the acceptance of responsibility for the home as a nation-building platform is all about.

Summary

Since parents have enormous influence in the roles of children in nation-building, we have only focused on fathers and mothers. However, children, especially the youths, are also expected to study, practice, teach and inspire nation-building. It is never too early to put the core nation-building values into action.

Another key point to note is this, in the process of active participation in nation-building fathers and mothers will also witness a transformation in character. This is a result of the demands of putting nation-building into action, in practice and teaching, which requires more of modelling through their lives than verbal communication. Therefore, both the parents and the children experience development in the family.

Potential Drawback of Development

One of the potential drawbacks in the development of a nation is the devaluing of the prominent role of the family. This is clearly observed in various developed nations where the prosperity that comes with the development of the nation, takes most fathers and even mothers away from the children for long periods of time. Their roles are handed over to the nannies, day care centres, nurseries, domestic staff, etc. It seems, when a nation is becoming prosperous, making of wealth takes priority over raising and sustaining a strong and stable family. So, to preserve the development of our nation for many generations, the importance of a strong family must be clearly and consistently advocated and pursued by all citizens. In summary, a strong, stable and nation-focused family is a prerequisite for building and sustaining a great nation.

chapter six

Foundation for Nation-Building: The Church

Church isn't where you meet. Church isn't a building.
Church is what you do. Church is who you are. Church
is the human outworking of the person of Jesus Christ.
Let's not go to church, let's be the church.
BRIDGET WILLARD

The second foundation for nation-building is the Faith. It is a good thing that Nigerians are known as religious people but we need to properly look at the role of Faith to ensure we fully identify with why it is one of the foundations for nation-building. I will be focusing on the role of the Church under faith in this chapter.

What is the Role of Church in Nation-building?

The missionary church made a huge contribution to the Nigerian society, especially in the areas of affordable education, healthcare and social welfare. The evidence of these abound around our country till date, not to mention that most of our pre and post independence generations were educated in missionary schools and born in missionary hospitals. These significant contributions to our nation cannot be ignored despite criticism of their doing little to openly challenge the social injustices of the colonial era, preferring instead to engage in quiet diplomacy with the colonial government rather than rocking the boat.

In the early years of independence, the Church continued to concentrate on her pre-colonial roles of providing affordable education, healthcare and social welfare, turning a blind eye to glaring social, political and economic injustices of the post independence era.

The end product was that the Church lost her foothold on her pre-colonial roles when government took over the running of schools and hospitals. In recent years, some states have handed some schools and hospitals back to the Church after years of neglect and lowered standard and several new generation churches have joined the traditional churches in setting up schools, clinics and social welfare programmes. However, these programmes are undertaken as add-on activities rather than core activities. As a result, the Church's contribution does not have far reaching impact.

I believe, the Church's primary mission on earth is to build a nation that is blessed (prosperous) and is a blessing to other nations, in so doing draw people to the God who works in and through us. The building of God's Kingdom is the same primary objective as the building of a nation - the growth and development of the people. It is in this regard that Michael Taylor declared, "For me Christianity is about the Kingdom, not about the church: it has to do with human growth and development not church growth and development". For the Church to fully identify with her role in nation-building, she must fully understand that her primary mission is to build the nation through investing resources — time, money and manpower — in the growth and development of the people.

A brief look at the background of the Church, how the Church originated will provide a better understanding of the role of the Church.

Genesis 12 tells us, "The LORD had said to Abram, "Leave your country, your people and your father's household and go to the land I will show you. I will make you into a great *nation* and I will bless you; I will make your name great, and you will be a blessing. I will bless those who bless you, and whoever curses you I will curse; and all people on earth will be blessed through you."

God's plan was to use one nation to bless all nations and that was to use the family of Abram (later called Abraham) to bless all the families of the earth (in the same vein, I believe God wants to use Nigeria to bless Africa). Out of Abraham descendents came a nation called Israel. God chose the nation of Israel to be the people that would go and teach others about Him. They would do this by modelling or living out the covenant relationship they had with God. This covenant included God's protection, provision and direction but it required faithfulness, accountability and responsibility from the people. When other nations witness the tremendous blessings upon Israel, they would be drawn into a loving relationship with their God. So God nurtured, protected, empowered and embraced his people and brought them into the land He had promised Abraham centuries before.

However, Israel failed in this task because they desired to be like the neighbouring nations and not the distinct people set apart to be used as a witness to the nations. They abandoned the covenant relationship and its commitments, and in its place got involved in the practices of their neighbours. They copied not just the religious practices and trust in these 'foreign' gods for deliverance when they encountered challenges but they desired to have the same monarchical government as their neighbours. In I Samuel 8:5, the elders of Israel on behalf of the people said "...now appoint a king to lead us, such as all the other nations have." By so doing, they rejected their special covenant relationship with God who governed them but preferred to be like the surrounding nations who had kings. A king who rule over them, lead them into battle and carry their responsibilities.

They got their desire in King Saul after God acknowledged their rejection. The result was the shift in responsibility from the people to their king and along went their reliance on God to dependence on the king.

It is important to note that God warned the nation of Israel about the consequences of their handing over responsibility to their king in I Samuel 8:11-18, "This is what the king who will reign over you will do: He will take your sons and make them serve with his chariots and horses, and they will run in front of his chariots. Some he will assign to be commanders of thousands and commanders of fifties, and others to plough his ground and reap his harvest, and still others to make weapons of war and equipment for his chariots. He will take your daughters to be perfumers and cooks and bakers. He will take the best of your fields and vineyards and olive groves and give them to his attendants. He will take a tenth of your grain and of your vintage and give it to his officials and attendants. Your menservants and maidservants and the best of your cattle and donkeys he will take for his own use. He will take a tenth of your flocks, and you yourselves will become his slaves. When that day comes, you will cry out for relief from the king you have chosen, and the Lord will not answer you in that day."

These warning did come to pass as kings after kings reined forcefully over the people (even the great kings like David and Solomon). But of even greater concern was that the people continued to fully delegate the responsibility and direction of their nation to their king. The end product was whatever their kings did, they did and for most of the time, their kings failed woefully, leading the nation of Israel to her collapse and consequent exile to other nations.

However, God's ultimate purpose for Israel — that of bringing the Messiah into the world — was fulfilled perfectly in the person of Jesus Christ. He arrived in Israel at a time when the people were forsaken, scattered all over the world and under Roman monarchy.

What Jesus came to achieve could not be seen by a people so set in their old ways which got them into trouble in the first place. To them, their salvation or deliverance lies in the promised Messiah who will come in the shape of a king. This king will be as great as his descendent king David and he will conquer and destroy all the occupiers of the land of Israel, restoring the glory of the nation like in the days of David and Solomon. Again, they placed the responsibility for their nation on a person and not on themselves.

Jesus came with a different message and approach. When he was thirty years old, He was ushered into His real ministry — His ministry as the Son of God, as the King who led differently. He called His apostles and revealed to them the will of the Father and that was the transfer of responsibility for the nation from the King back to the people. He effectively started the process of nation-building all over again by transferring the responsibility for the nation from Him, the Messiah, back to the people. The salvation or deliverance of the nation was not to be found in the king who, to be honest, will rule for just a limited period of time and would not allow the people to be responsible or accountable for the building and sustenance of their nation. Salvation will be found in the people of that nation taking personal responsibility for their actions and then accepting His kingship to become part of God's kingdom, both in the spirit and then physically. This was his message.

To build this new kingdom or nation, he chose 12 disciples whom he taught the kingdom principles, starting with putting the destiny of the nation in their hands. To pave the way for the manifestation of these 'kingdom citizens', he allowed Himself to be killed by crucifixion on the cross and on the third day, he resurrected to establish the sovereignty of His kingdom for eternity.

His departure, rapture into heaven 40 days after resurrection, did not lead to the end of His dynasty as is the case with kings, who carried the responsibility of the people, His kingdom exploded as His 'citizens' took up responsibility for building the kingdom with the aid of His Spirit. That kingdom blossomed and transform into a body now called the church with members from every tribe and tongue and this happened despite severe persecution against His kingdom by the Romans and many others groups since then.

This is a kingdom that is still growing in number and influence with the ultimate goal of reigning with the King for eternity. In the meantime, the King (Jesus) continues to call His citizens to focus on human growth and development emphasizing personal responsibility for our soul and for the nation as the basis (not delegating it to leaders, government or church). Her [Church] impact has been felt around the world in the over 2000 year of existence and a good example of these is seen in western nations with strong Christian heritage being the most developed nations of the world today.

Having seen how the Church came about and continues to operate, it is inevitable that she must be in the forefront of any activity that is focused on human growth and development — from education, to healthcare, to sports, to social work, to politics, to advocacy, to mobilization, etc. I believe, only then, can it be said that the Church exist in Nigeria as here lies the role of the Church in nation-building.

It is also important to note that the Church started with the same nation-building implementation steps — Study, Practice, Teach and Inspire.

Why the Church?

I have used the origin of the Church to define her role in nation-building but that in itself is not enough to get the Church to lead the efforts to build our nation. We need to go further to ask why the Church should play a leading role and in the process reveal the motivation for the Church. The dual purpose is to ensure the Church leadership fully identifies with her role and that her members hold the leaders accountable in this regard.

Here are the keys reasons:

It is the mandate of the Church to build

As stated earlier, the primary mission of the Church is to build a nation that is blessed and is a blessing. The building of a nation is the growth and development of her people. This entails bringing people to the knowledge of Jesus (winning souls) and then building their lives (character development through nation-building core values impartation). It is this transformation in the life of a Kingdom citizen that results in the transformation of the nation. So, the mandate to build the kingdom does not only have spiritual manifestations but also physical manifestations and the benefits are to both 'citizens' of the Kingdom and those outside. Nation-building is a natural fit for the Church as it aligns with her mandate.

The Church was created for the benefit of others: As best expressed by William Temple, "A church is the only organization that exists primarily for the benefit of non-members." The Church was created to use her influence and resources for the benefit of the nation. Her anointing, spiritual gifts, finances, human resources (members), influence (members in government, international organisations) and all other resources are for the care, growth and development of the people, both members and non-members.

The message of the Church

The core messages of the Church are essentially messages that builds a nation. These are messages that form the basis of nation-building core values. Messages of compassion, love God and your neighbour; of responsibility, for your salvation and your nation; of opportunity, to be all God had created us and others to be; of valour, given by God's spirit to confront and change the tide of underdevelopment; of liberty, from sin and human oppression; of equality, before God and with man; of enterprise, God-given potential to achieve great things; of unity, of the church and of the nation; of ability, as a wonderful and capable creation of God; and of spirituality, the worship of God and faith in His ability to use us to bring about change. A nation rises or falls based on her values and through her messages, the Church holds the key for providing and sustaining the proper framework (values) for our development.

The influence of the Church

Nigerians are known to be religious people with a significant number of our population professing to be Christians or Muslims. Nigerians do not only profess to be religious but are quite passionate about attendance of religious gatherings. As a result, the strong pull of the church does make her the biggest influence in our society. Church leaders are well respected, sometimes revered, by members, non-members and even people in government. This is because they are known as the messengers of the God, a channel for God to communicate with His people. But it is this immense influence that the Church has on her members, many of whom hold positions of importance in the nation, that is of note. Such influence should be used to mobilize members to action and to instil in them values that build the nation. Since the Church exerts the strongest influence in our nation, she is the key vehicle for change.

The large human resources of the Church

The Church has at its disposal a huge human resources: her members. When you consider that membership of some churches exceeds that of any employer of labour, including the government, and these members regularly attend church meetings, are very committed to church programmes and vision, and are quite loyal to the church leadership, you will realise the Church has a unique advantage.

Enormous financial resources of the Church

One of the products of her influence on her large and mostly dedicated human resources and on international organisations is an enormous financial resource. This comes in the form of regular tithes, offerings, gifts and grants, most of which are tax free. The Church in Nigeria has the added benefit of not paying government taxes on her financial resources but at the same time, they can earn bank interest from their income. Therefore, the Church is well equipped to lead nation-building with her financial resources, remembering that she was created for the benefit of others.

The Role of the Church in Nation-Building

The role of the Church in nation-building starts within the Church where the work of the Kingdom is not left to the leadership but every member takes responsibility to build their temple through righteous living and His temple by engaging in the works of His Church. The Church leadership needs to awaken members to this responsibility and the Church members need to engage the leadership about involving more members in works of the Church.

Through the study, practice and teaching of nation-building, the Church can and should pull on its mandate, influence and enormous resources to build the nation in these key areas:
- **Prayer and Fasting**
- **Messaging**
- **Training**
- **Healthcare**
- **Social Work**
- **Advocacy**
- **Mobilisation**

Prayer and Fasting

For the Church, everything starts at the place of prayer therefore her role in nation-building must start with prayer. The Church believes in the power of prayer to enable change in whatever circumstance because prayer is the means of communicating with God and an invitation to Him to intervene in human affairs. That being the case, the Church must take the development and preservation of our nation as one of her key petitions to God. She must not only do this as a corporate body, at church services, but must encourage her members to do this regularly on individual basis, at their individual prayer time.

What are the key prayer points for the church?

The Church is commanded to pray for people in leadership, in authority, in order for us to reap the benefits of good governance, justice, peace and righteousness. The call to pray for our leaders is not only a command but also a responsibility. The agenda of her meeting has to consistently incorporate a time set aside to pray for:

Family Leadership: Since the family is the foundation of any society, prayers for parents, especially fathers, must be offered. That God will protect and encourage parents. Also, that God will make the institution of fatherhood and motherhood stronger and much desired to Nigerians.

Political Leadership: Executive and Legislative arms of government: That the fear of God will be sown into their hearts which will result in servant leadership (serving the people instead of themselves with humility). That God will give them the vision and the courage to build the nation with total commitment and passion.

The Judiciary: That they will recognise their crucial role in eliminating injustice and protecting the equality and liberty of the people.

Traditional Rulers: That they will use their position to unite the people and ensure the development of the community

Religious Leaders: That they will remember that their commitment is not only to God but to man. That they will dedicate their time and resources to the development of Nigeria

Heads of Commerce and Industry: That business will be conducted with a patriotic spirit and integrity. That the spirit of ambition and enterprise will be tempered by the spirit of compassion and responsibility

Unity of our nation: One of the key challenges facing our nation is the lack of acceptance of Nigeria, by many of her people, due to how she was created. However, the unity of the country is essential to her development and acceptance of God's plan for Nigeria is an important key to this. Thus, the Church needs to focus her prayers on the unity of the country. Also, the Church needs to pray for God's intervention on issues that threaten our unity such as the electoral fraud, ethnicity, political structure, religion conflicts, etc.

Educational System: Since Education has been determined as the bedrock for nation-building, it is important for the Church to focus her prayers on it. Prayers are required for head of schools, teachers, students and the government supervisory agencies. We need to seek God's intervention in the restoration of discipline, academic excellence by students and teachers, educational opportunity for the less privileged, and so on.

Families: The family provides the perfect platform for the study, practice and teaching of nation-building. In addition, a strong and stable family determines the strength and stability of a nation. Therefore, it is pertinent for the church to pray for the strengthening of the family structure, Fathers, Mothers, children and extended family, that each will rise to their responsibility with full commitment and dedication.

Core Values: Having established the importance of the nation-building core values in transforming our thoughts, words and action, it is important for the church to pray for all Nigerians to imbibe and exhibit these values in public and in private.

It must be noted that prayer for the nation should not be an add-on activity but must be made one of the primary activities of the church. Focused prayer on the nation will result in a shift from a self focused church to nation focused church in thoughts, words and actions. Prayer is essential in nation-building because it not only communicates our needs to God but it also prepares us to become His tool to build the nation.

Messaging

The second primary role of the Church is in the messages that she preaches to her members. We have recognized that due to her spiritual authority, her message carries enormous weight with its large membership. So, the Church must utilize this opportunity to preach messages that will transform the thoughts, words and actions of her members from being self-focused to nation-focused.

The Church has not only the influence to achieve this but the added motivation that this is her mandate from God. Many churches are known to hold several meetings in a week and these are well attended by her members. Nation-building messages can be delivered and reiterated from the pulpit on a regular basis. By using scriptures to support these messages, most members will witness character transformation which will result in the transformation of our nation. These nation-building sermons are not separate from the true message of the gospel. Focus has to shift from the emphasis on prosperity (self seeking) to preaching servant hood , (serving others) because the core of Jesus' teaching was that he did not come to be served but to serve and to give His life as a ransom for many. The Bible further stated that we should likewise lay down our lives for others and in so doing, follow the example of Jesus.

The key issues the Church needs to consistently teach are:

Responsibility: For our actions, our families and our communities and the nation. Change begins from a place of responsibility and the Church must preach about this. Learning from her origin, she needs to teach her members that change is in our hands and not in the hands of our government.

Love: The greatest commandment given by Jesus – The love of God and of man. This sort of love expresses itself in sacrificial acts of compassion. True compassion is manifested when we give up our comfort, convenience, desires, to implement change in the lives of others.

God's Plan: God's plan is to bless Nigeria and use her to bless other nations around the world, especially in Africa. If the Church states that God is a good God and that He can turn a mistake into something good, she has to believe and teach that God's plans for Nigeria is to prosper her, making good out of the mistake in her creation.

Nation-building Core Values: These are values that we must hold and express daily. Not only must the Church teach nation-building core values but she must commit resources to the establishment, the practice and the sustenance of these values, as well as, preach against the negative values that has held us captive for too long. The Church's role in building good character in her members is possible through the teaching of the core values. The Church must note that she ceases to exist in her true form when these core values become non-existent.

Patriotism: The church should instil pride and passion for the nation into her members through her messages. Such messages should include consistent prayer for the nation, her leaders, her peacekeepers in foreign mission and the promotion of our symbols of nationhood, Anthem, Flag, Pledge, etc.

Volunteering: To accomplish the enormous task of building a nation, much of the work would have to be done by volunteering. This involves people volunteering their time, expertise, training, experience and other resources to achieve a nation-building objective. The Church's message should seek to encourage members and non-members to volunteer for at least one project.

Training

Training is a key element used by the Church to execute her

mandate to save and transform lives. Through biblical training, the Church enables people to become informed, liberated, enlightened, empowered and equipped to go and be all God had created them to be. As part of her nation-building role, the church has to also make other forms of t raining a focal point of her nation-building activities. Nelson Mandela said, "Education is the most powerful weapon which you can use to change the world."

Such training includes:

Conventional Education: By this we mean, school education which ranges from Primary to Secondary schools and Tertiary Institutions. Out of these three, I believe the Church's focus should be on primary and secondary school education because a nation stand or falls on the strength of her primary and secondary school education. This is the foundation that we build our nation upon. At the still-born stage of our development, it is imperative that this task is not left to government alone (this is not the case even in developed nations) but it also requires the Church to take a leading role with the commitment of a large percentage of her resources.

As this is the foundation that builds a nation, it should not be dominated by the private sector, developed nations do not have this model neither did they become developed through this approach. So, first class primary education should be provided for free by the Church, with first class secondary school education being made available at an affordable rate. Affordable would mean a rate that the majority of her members can afford. The Church must also educate parents on the importance of education to ensure 100% commitment by parents and students. The Church would also have the right footing to institute discipline in schools and teach nation-building values. The focus of her educational training should not be the emancipated of the educated only but also emancipation of others by those they educate.

Specialist Training: The Church must also focus on the establishment of qualitative and affordable teacher training colleges to train and equip teachers who will teach in the primary and secondary schools. These teachers will not only learn excellent and up to date teaching techniques but will be equipped with the spirit of service which will make them see their vocation as more of a service than a job.

Still part of specialist training and as part of her mandate to meet the needs of all groups, privileged and underprivileged, the Church should also invest her resources in the establishment of schools for children with disabilities because the Church knows, they are created by God and being alive, they [disabled children] also have a purpose to accomplish.

Also in this category are schools for Adult Education, Technical and Vocational training. This is how the Church would ensure that boys, girls, children with disabilities, adults who missed out on education, people with more interest in technical or vocational training and every other educational needs are properly catered for.

The Church should go even further in the area of training. She has to be involved in the setting up and running of youth/sports clubs, character building groups: Girls Guides, Boys Brigade and Boys Scout. This sort of engagements provides another platform to impart nation-building values in the children, the nation-builders of tomorrow's society.

At this stage of our development, I believe tertiary institutions should not be the focus of the church. Not only because the enormous capital required will shift focus from primary and secondary education but also because an undeveloped nation like ours can only absorb roughly 5-10% of its university graduates. This means, the nation is in desperate need of a majority with qualitative educational foundation in primary and secondary schools, and also specialist schools.

Nation-building requires that our education system should be able to produce 16-18 year olds with quality primary and secondary school education, who have acquired life/Vocational/Technical skills and values, are good disciples and are equipped to go into the workforce or set up their own ventures. To achieve this, I believe the church should focus solely in this sector and limit their involvement in Tertiary Institution to advocacy and occasional research sponsorship. With her full commitment to the education of the 5 – 18 year olds (both conventional and specialist), she can ensure the acceleration of quality result and the undivided attention given will lead to more research and innovative ways to educate our children. Children should be one of the focal point of our nation-building activities because through them, we create the future we desire for our nation, and training is the primary tool to achieve this.

Illiteracy is a menace. The Church must not only preach against it but must be actively involved in eliminating it to produce a developed nation which will also spread development to every part of Africa and the rest of the world. This will be fulfilling God's plan for our nation Nigeria.

Healthcare

One of the central themes of Jesus' ministry was healing the sick. In Luke 9:1-2, Jesus sent out His disciples to preach the Kingdom and to heal the sick. If this is true of Jesus, it must be true of His church. One of the primary objectives of the Church should be making available healthcare facilities and the impartation of good health values.

I recommend healthcare mission should be in the following areas:

Treatment: The Church should invest in the establishment of hospitals, health centres and mobile clinics. But more than that, the church must make these establishments affordable and accessible. During colonial days, the missionaries discovered that the emancipation of our people through education was frequently interrupted by health challenges and so their response was to set up hospitals to preserve lives. They knew the people were poor but that did not stop them from investing huge resources to get the hospitals established and equipped, staff trained, doctors brought in, transportation provided and more importantly, most of the services were free. There lies a model the Church today should emulate.

Our nation requires health centres and mobile clinics for primary health care but also hospitals that provides specialist services such as Emergency services, physiotherapy, care for patients with eye problems, dental problems, cancer, HIV/Aids, diabetes, leprosy, mental illness, etc.

Nigeria is losing large numbers of her citizens, and many die in their prime, due to lack of affordable healthcare and irrespective of government policies and actions, the Church must be led by compassion to not only save the situation but take a lead role as part of her nation-building activities. She cannot afford to leave the establishment and management of health centres and hospitals solely in the hands of government and the private sector, especially at this stage of our development

Maternity and Child Health: Besides ministering to the sick through her involvement in the running of hospitals and health centres, the church must also take the lead role in maternity and child healthcare.

This ministry should involve:

- The setting up of maternity clinics in hospitals, health centres, church premises, community centres and town halls, mobile clinics, etc.
- Provision of free prenatal, natal and postnatal care such as medical checkups, baby scans, delivery facilities, baby clothing, medications (for mother and baby), immunization, baby cots, mosquito nets, baby milk, etc.
- Training, educating women and men through prenatal and postnatal classes, leaflets, home visits and relevant church ministry e.g., Womb ministry.
- The establishment and management of motherless babies homes for the care of abandoned babies

In August 2009, The Executive Director of United Nations

Children's Fund (UNICEF), Ann Venemana, said at a ministerial press briefing on World Breastfeeding and Child Health week, held in Abuja, that infant mortality rate in Nigeria is unacceptably high. This is one of the clearest indicators of an undeveloped nation; Hence, the church must arise to her calling because if we fail to care for the children, who are gifts from God, we would have failed in every other thing.

Pharmacy: One of the biggest challenges in our nation is the availability and affordability of genuine medication. This is a problem faced by not only the less privileged but also those in the middle and upper classes. I think it is fair to say that majority of church members are concerned about this. In addition to the provision of hospitals, health centres and maternity clinics, the Church should be involved in the establishment and management of pharmacies that will provide good quality medication at an affordable price. The Church will help to drastically reduce the number of deaths and medical complications caused by fake medication or the lack of or high cost of medication.

Training: Healthcare is not only about infrastructures but also about the personnel. As the Church is involved in training programmes for children and Adults, she must incorporate specialist training for the health sector. As stated under her role in training, the objective is to produce medical personnel who will see their vocation as a service rather than a job or duty.

The success of the Church's healthcare efforts will be determined by the dedication of her staff and the dedication of the staff will be determined by the training given by Church owned medical training schools. These schools will strengthen medical teachings with biblical teachings on service and in the process produce the Florence Nightingales of our nation. I really believe the church should give more attention to the area of training nurses, midwives and care workers. This is because the main work in the provision of healthcare is undertaken by this group and their commitment is crucial to the success of our healthcare i.e., the survival of our people.

Health Values: The Church should undertake extensive health campaigns to educate Nigerians on proper health values and immunizations. This could be in the form of messages during and after church meetings, road shows to towns and villages, production and distribution of health leaflets, etc. The Church is well aware that many Nigerians, including her members, suffer health problems due to ignorance and most of these problems could have been avoided with sufficient information.

Research: To encourage innovations in our healthcare systems, the church should invest in medical researches. She can play a lead role in funding research into issues like the treatment and prevention of killer diseases like malaria. According to UNICEF report on Partnering to roll back malaria in Bauchi State, dated 22nd April 2009, malaria kills 250,000 Nigerian children under the age of 5 each year and it is responsible for about 66 per cent of all hospital/clinic visits in Nigeria (the disease affects five times as many people as HIV/AIDS, leprosy, measles and tuberculosis). As the leading killer of our people, not only children, the Church has to seize the initiative in finding lasting solutions to this epidemic through investment in medical research. This medical research can be initiated by the Church alone or in partnership with the private sector or our universities. Other areas of research could include new drugs, sickle cell, healthcare service delivery, nutrition, etc.

As summed up by former British Prime Minister, Benjamin Disraeli, "The health of the people is really the foundation upon which all their happiness and all their powers as a state depend." Good healthcare service is one of the main foundations for building and sustaining a great nation.

Social Work

Whilst the focus on training is to engineer the emancipation of the people and the focus on health is to improve the wellbeing of the people and preserve lives, the focus on social work is to protect the worth and improve the opportunities of the most vulnerable, less privileged and socially disadvantaged. This also is a cardinal theme of the Church, as she is called to minister to the needs of those neglected by society and this ministry is urgently needed as the economic hardship in our nation has increased the number of such persons.

I would categorise the key needs as Rehabilitation, Care Homes, Community Development and Emergency Relief Services:

Rehabilitation Work: Many churches have missionary teams that visit prisons and work in the area of rehabilitation of addicts. But in nation-building the Church is required to take a more prominent role. This involves setting up rehabilitation centres for ex-prisoners, drug addicts, sex workers, child slaves, etc. These centres should not be created as 'pity centres' but a place where people can be trained, equipped and released to go give back into the nation. They have to come out of such centres rehabilitated and with a feeling of their God-given worth. These would not only reduce the level of crime in our nation but will become a vehicle for transforming the lives of people without hope. It is the Church that should carry this burden and demonstrate that these are not second class citizens and that God gives each one of us more than a second chance.

Care Homes: In addition to focusing on rehabilitation, the church must also be actively involved in the setting up and managing of orphanages, old peoples homes and homes for the disabled. In our current state, we have a lot of orphans, elderly people and the disabled who does not receive support from government, nor, in many cases, from their families. As a result, they are abandoned on streets and ignored by

Nigerians. The church is duty bound to ensure the care of these vulnerable Nigerians. Again, these are not second class citizens and as such, do not require pity but compassion and opportunity.

This is why the Church needs to invest in setting up and running well managed homes for these categories of people and thus, provide opportunities for them to reach their God-given potential. The Church should also support our aged citizens (many of whom contributed in one way or the other to building our nation).

Community Development: Another area of social work for the Church in nation-building is community development. The Church is not located in the air but in a community and her members are from the community. Therefore, the Church must get involved in community development projects that would affect the lives of her members, her host community and disadvantaged communities. The beauty of community development projects is that it involves a lot of volunteering by church members and members of the benefiting community, both of whom are sufficiently available.

Some key areas of focus should include Water, Sanitation, Social Housing, Micro Finance Schemes and Job Creation.

Water: Where proper water infrastructure is lacking, the Church should take the lead in providing borehole and water tanks in their neighbouring communities, schools, care and rehabilitation homes. This will drastically reduce many diseases caused by bad water and it would also assist those poor families who can't afford to buy water from available boreholes.

Sanitation: The Church should not only teach members and the community about the importance of good sanitation but she must also get involved in the process. This she can do by setting aside regular dates in their calendar to undertake sanitation exercises and enlightenment.

Social Housing: Using volunteers, from members and

benefiting community, the Church can make significant impact in the area of social housing. Obviously, attention would be given to the housing needs of the vulnerable and less privileged like widows left with no inheritance, pensioners and disabled. The Church can also invest in providing housing for teachers and healthcare workers at their schools and hospitals and also provide social housing for their host community. Sometimes, what is required is not just the building of simple affordable housing but also the upgrading poorly built homes.

Micro Finance Schemes: Still part of her community development efforts, the Church must be actively involved in providing micro finance to members who are looking to establish small businesses but are constrained by lack of resources. With the reverence most members have for the church, they are most likely to manage the Church's micro finance better than a bank loan. This is in addition to the added benefit that such schemes will likely come with affordable interest rates.

Job Creation: The church can use her community development activities as a means for job creation.

Emergency Relief Services: Emergencies and natural disasters are inevitable in any society and due to climate change there are more earthquakes, flooding, heat wave and drought around the globe. In our nation, disasters also do occur as a result of epidemic and political, religious or communal conflicts. The Church has to have a proactive approach to these issues and not only a reactionary approach. That means, the Church should set up a unit that is trained, equipped with the right materials to properly and promptly address any emergencies. As often discovered, money is not normally the immediate solution in times of emergencies but having the manpower, equipment and materials to address the urgent needs of the victims.

Emergency relief service is not a role that should be left to the Nigerian Red Cross or National Emergency Management

Agency (NEMA). The Church has a key role to play here as she is in the best position to minister to both the physical and spiritual needs of the victims. This becomes essential when the victims have to go through a long recovery process as it is the case in such situation.

Advocacy

Advocacy is mainly about engaging or lobbying those with the apparatus of power to effect change in required areas. The purpose is to influence change in society, whether it is appealing to an individual about their behaviour, employers about their rules or the government about their laws. According to a paper from leading UK relief and development charity Tearfund on *The mission of the church and the role of Advocacy* by Graham Gordon and Bryan Evans,

> involvement in advocacy is vital, both practically and theologically, to the church's calling to bring about justice, speak for truth, defend the poor and oppressed, and to work to redeem the whole creation. Advocacy involves both tackling individual cases of injustice or poverty, and tackling systems and structures that allow this injustice to happen. Advocacy is firmly rooted in the hope and promise we have for a better future and we do it in the confidence that God is working His purposes out.

The Church is about the nation-building values we discussed in the third chapter and those values form the basis of what she advocates for. As part of her nation-building role, the Church must use her strong voice with her convictions, to advocate in these areas and this list is nowhere conclusive:

Fight against Corruption: It is well known fact that our nation is one of the most corrupt nations in the world and corruption runs deep in the society. There is no facet of our society that has been exempted by this malaise. The Church must speak out against corruption publicly, and privately in consultation with government representatives. She must also be involved in reporting corruption cases and mounting pressure on relevant government agencies and the judiciary to ensure thorough investigation and prosecution are carried out. The church must act as a watchdog to ensure that the every Nigerian is treated equally before the law. After, all, the Church believes we are created equally by God.

Fight against Poverty: It is the Church's role to ensure that the hardship Nigerians are facing is impressed upon our political leaders. This she can do by speaking out, from the pulpit, in the press, in private consultations with government representatives, and by undertaking research on poverty and then lobbying government with the findings to ensure implementation.

Fight against injustice: One of the sad effects of our underdevelopment is the regular signs of injustice. It could range from regional underdevelopment — like in the Niger Delta region to false imprisonment, lack of deserved compensation, owed salaries and pensions, oppression by those in government, unfair trial from the law courts, long awaiting trial period in prisons, etc. The Church should be a place where people can bring their complaints and be heard. Not only be heard but be defended. She is the place of hope and that must include hope for those faced with injustice. That means, the Church must invest her resources to fight injustice suffered by the people.

Reforms: The Church has to be involved in the lobbying of members of the legislative and executive arms of government to enable changes in our Electoral law and process, Security agencies operation and funding, Education, Health and Social funding and reforms. Again, her role in advocacy should involve offering well researched options that will bring positive change.

Health Epidemics: The Church should also be involved in influencing government and its agencies attitude to health epidemics. These could be HIV/AIDs, polio, malaria, cholera, etc. She needs to seek increased government funding, training, expansion of services, innovative ways to treatment, prevention and the increased visibility for the victims to ensure the epidemic is better understood by government and the general society.

Environment: Since the Church believes that the Earth was created by God, she must be in the forefront of advocacy for the environment. Our nation is daily faced with environmental damage and pollution due to rapid unplanned urbanization, overpopulation, oil spillage, car emissions, industrial waste, erosion, deforestation, desertification, etc. What is worse about our situation is that the nation is focused on provision of basic infrastructure and reduction of poverty with little or no concern for environmental impact on lives. This is why the church must lead this initiative to educate, inform and influence our policy makers, policy implementers, manufacturers and the general public about the urgency of the situation and, the actions that must be taken.

It is important to note that the authenticity or legitimacy of the Church's advocacy activities would be dependent upon her activities in nation-building. For example, if she is investing financial and human capital in the educational sector, she would have a stronger voice to advocate educational reforms through private and public lobbying. In effect, the church must lead by example.

Mobilisation

This is the act of mobilising the Church leadership and the congregation to undertake nation-building activities. A key element because it is the effective mobilization of her members that would determine the level of her success in nation-building activities. We stated earlier that the Church's huge human resources (members) is a major strength and it is these members who would be mobilized through discipleship i.e., getting them involved in the ministry — the activities of the church.

As part of her nation-building role, the Church should actively mobilise in these key areas:

Her Activities: The Church should first mobilise her members to invest their resources, time, expertise, finances, skills, etc., in nation-building activities: prayer for the nation, training, healthcare, social work and advocacy.

Government Policies: The Church should mobilise support for government policies that would benefit the people, like immunisation, free primary and secondary education, payment of taxes, etc.

Electoral Process: She should also be involved in mobilising members to participate in the electoral process. This could be coming forward as candidates, forming political parties or exercising their civil right by voting.

Volunteering: The Church has the scriptural backing and the natural influence to cause members to volunteer themselves for nation-building activities. The free offer of members time, influence and expertise would make a significant difference in the Church's involvement in building a great nation. In addition, it would cause members to apply this same approach in other areas of society and in the process, enable and foster an environment where people are laying down their lives for others. Volunteering will enable the Church achieve quite a lot with her current financial resources.

Civil Disobedience: When necessary, the Church may mobilise members to undertake civil disobedience to achieve a positive change in our nation. This tool may be called into action where a government policy or form of governance is inflicting severe pain on majority of Nigerians. Civil disobedience, such as protest march, boycott, etc., have played key roles in bringing about significant change in many nations of the world today and several were led by the Church.

The Church can mobilise her members through her messaging, formation of church target groups, prayer, discipleship (making church the business of the members and not only the leadership).

Summary

It was the Church that initiated the establishment and spread of the primary and secondary schools, for boys and quite significantly for girls, in Nigeria during the pre and post independence era. It could be claimed that the takeover of schools, hospitals and care homes by the government in 1976, minimised the impact of the Church in these sectors and the benefits for the nation. But it can also be added that most churches have over the years ignored the urgent need to take responsibility for these sectors and when they did, they came on board as a private sector organization catering to the needs of the privileged few which did not account for up to 20% of their congregation. Now is the time for the church to cater to the needs of majority in the society, the sort of people Jesus came for and they will find that this is about 80% of members.

The role of the Catholic Church in nation-building must be commended. They have a long history of providing education, healthcare, social work, advocacy and mobilisation. There have also been activities by other churches including Pentecostals but again what is needed is for these nation-building efforts to be addressed as a primary activity rather than an add-on activity. These will result in focus of the Church's efforts on a larger number of Nigerians and not just a privileged few.

The primary role of the church is to study, practice, teach and inspire Jesus' model of servanthood by creating an atmosphere and ministry which lays emphasis on service to society. Here lies the key reason why the church should play a leading role in nation-building. It is also the role of church members to hold their leadership accountable at each stage of the process and the role of the church leadership to ensure members are fully mobilised and committed to the process.

Building the Kingdom of God is synonymous with building

the nation. This is because the Kingdom building activities are the same as nation building activities i.e., transformation of soul, change of focus from self to others, change of values, use of God's gifts for the benefit of others with a spirit of excellence, care for the less privileged, etc. Jesus called His Church to build the Kingdom and if His Kingdom people answer His call, they will build the nation.

If the Church will not rise up to fulfil her role in nation-building, inevitably, the vacuum created will lead to loss of current influence. The case study on William Booth and the Salvation Army in the next chapter is a good example of the impact a church can make.

chapter seven

Case study of Nation-Building

That some achieve great success, is proof to all that others can achieve it as well.
ABRAHAM LINCOLN

The purpose of this final chapter is to prove the ideal of nation-building is also a reality. We shall do this by highlighting a few case studies or stories of people who passed through the stages of nation-building and the impact of their contribution to the development of their nation.

These are stories of ordinary people who were confronted with situations that are similar to, if not worse than, what we are facing in our nation. They studied the situation and came up with a plan of what they could do. As that was not enough, they risked everything to manifest their transformed thoughts through their words and actions. These words and actions reflected in their practicing and teaching what they were fully committed to. The result was that they inspired many others into becoming nation-builders.

A case study is chosen for each key area of development — education, healthcare, church, civil Rights, politics and social welfare. Each case study is an excellent example of the core nation-building values at work. I am hopeful that these individuals and institutions would inspire us to effect nation-building within our area of influence, using the abilities, skills, experiences and contacts at our disposal.

Education

We believe that education is the great enabler [and that] it's the foundation for life opportunity. From my vantage point, we're working to enable our country to live up to its ideals... of ensuring that all of our kids have the chance at the American Dream.

WENDY KOPP

Background History

Wendy Kopp was born 29th June 1967 and was raised in a comfortable white middle class neighborhood in Dallas, Texas. Due to her privileged background, Kopp benefitted from a quality educational system where she was an excellent student.

In 1985, she gained admission into the prestigious Princeton University and graduated with a bachelor's degree in public policy. It was during her time at Princeton that Kopp came to realise that the educational opportunities she enjoyed was not accessible to Americans from poor backgrounds. The sharing of student accommodation with a student from New York's poorest and most disadvantaged school district enabled her appreciate the challenges faced by children from poor background with poor educational system.

This discovery got her involved in an organisation that brought together Princeton students and the local business leaders to discuss social issues. The organisation was called the Foundation of Student Communication and she led it. While running the organisation she discovered that several of her colleagues were interested in addressing social issues and many were interested in teaching. Thus she was to develop a national Teacher Corps for young graduates, similar to the Peace Corps.

Kopp used the opportunity of presenting a thesis for her degree to develop this concept. She put together a detailed plan for an organisation that would recruit the most talented young college graduates, train them and post them to underserved school in challenging districts as teachers and inspiration to the unmotivated students.

In 1989, after her graduation, at the age of just 22 years but with a vision, Kopp turned her thesis into the organisation called Teach for America (TFA). Her vision was to ensure that "one day, all children in our nation will have the opportunity to attain an excellent education" (Kopp, 2001: 174). 489 people became the first batch of recruits selected from 2,500 applicants. By 2010, with 7,300 active recruits, the organisation received over 35,000 applications for recruitment. This included graduates from prestigious universities like Harvard, Princeton, MIT, every one of them keen to make a difference in the lives of at-risk students, for less money and fame, but for greater impact.

Kopp's vision and the impact of Teach for America is seen in the numerous foundations and federal agencies that consistently support their activities with grants.

Contribution to nation-building

No doubt, America is a developed nation and a superpower but it also has its educational challenges and Wendy Kopp's TFA has played a significant role in improving educational standard by seeking to make quality education available to kids from poor backgrounds. This is done to ensure that America maintains her leadership role in the global community, as she continues to produce educated citizens with the capacity to achieve their dreams and visions. It is important to note that improving educational standard was seen in the light of its benefit for the nation, which of course included the individual student.

How did Wendy Kopp's Teach for America improve Educational Standards?

Complements teaching staff numbers: The key focus of TFA is to recruit and train graduates from prestigious colleges on a two year service, to serve as teachers to inner city and rural areas where there are acute teacher shortages. Due to the shortages in these communities, the educational standard are normally quite low and this produces poorly educated children.

Targets areas with poor educational system: Not only does TFA seek to complement teaching staff numbers but it also targets areas with poor educational system thereby, bridging the educational gap in the country. The organisation's emphasis is to target areas with poor schools with the goal of improving educational standards, in the process, transforming not only the students but the community.

The teachers mentor and inspire students: Another key contribution to improving educational standard is the mentoring and inspiration that TFA teachers provide to the disadvantaged students. Since the teachers are mostly fresh graduates from top American colleges, their good academic achievements, youthfulness and intelligence creates the profile required to obtain a response from the mostly disenchanted students. Consequently, many students are inspired to commit more time to their studies, go to school early, study late and even on weekends. It also provides the teachers with the time to accelerate the progress of the children's education and show them evidence of their potential, if they work hard enough. The teacher's mentoring is not limited to educational studies but also extends to helping the students and their families combat negative social factors deeply rooted in their communities.

Teach for America (TFA) views teaching as a social call: For many young, bright graduates with the energy and passion to make a difference in the world, TFA provides that platform and the mechanism to get involved in tackling the socio-economic challenges of rural and inner-city communities. Most of these graduates from top American colleges could easily secure quality jobs but take two years off to help build their community and in extension, their nation. These teachers encounter with the other side of America inspires in them [the teachers] the desire to actively become involved in the American educational system. That inspiration results in their becoming permanent teachers and administrators or becoming indirectly involved through educational reforms advocacy in the public and private sectors.

Rigorous Recruitment Process: A key reason for the impact TFA has made in improving educational standard is due to the quality of her teachers and that is a result of the rigorous recruitment process involved in getting the teachers. The TFA intensive recruitment efforts includes actively targeting seniors at the nation's top colleges and universities, with a special focus on attracting maths and science majors, and making particular effort to encourage applications from ethnic minorities. TFA programme remains very selective as the organisation receives over 35,000 applications but recruited only 7,300. While TFA teachers have exceptional academic records, the recruitment process also seeks out teachers with the experience, drive, and commitment to become leaders beyond the classroom.

Intensive Training Programme: New teacher training begins with extensive curriculum review and observation of public school classes during the spring of corps members' senior year. The summer after graduation includes an intensive five-week training programme that entails teaching summer school under the close supervision of experienced teachers. Once in the classroom, TFA continues to promote the professional development of teachers through ongoing technical support, training, and evaluation by regional TFA staff. TFA teachers are also required to enrol in teacher certification programs in their local jurisdictions. TFA also actively researches the effectiveness of their teachers and training programmes.

TFA essentially shifts the 'me' factor in this energetic bunch of graduates recruits to the 'others' factor and at the same time, it presents the true state of the American society to those who will lead the nation in the near future.

In a 2004 Mathematical Policy Research report by Paul T.

Decket, Daniel P. Mayer and Steven Glazerman titled *The Effects of Teach for America on Students: Findings from a National Evaluation*, the central findings stated "After one year, students taught by TFA teachers outperformed students in control classrooms ... TFA teachers outperformed not only other novice teachers but also veteran and certified teachers in the same schools."

The impact of Teach for America on that country's educational system is immense especially when we consider that about two-thirds of her teachers continue in the educational field after their two year service. Over 400 alumni of TFA are school principals, several others are district education superintendents, teachers, educational administrators and those in the corporate world have been noted to actively support the organisation's funding requirements.

Today, Teach for America model is being exported to other countries in Europe, South America, Australia and Asia under the organisation "Teach for All". Hopefully, we can see something similar implemented in Nigeria because our educational system is in urgent need of such assistance.

Healthcare

One measure of civilization is, how well do we treat the most vulnerable members of our society?

WILLIAM H. FOEGE

Background History

William Foege was born 12th March 1936 in Decorah, Iowa, USA, the third of six children born to a Lutheran minister. Two main inspirations in his life were his uncle who was a Lutheran missionary to New Guinea and his childhood hero, Dr. Albert Schweitzer, who went to Africa to treat the poor (he read Albert Schweitzer's autobiography, *The Primeval Forest* as a boy). Based on these influence, he desired, as a teenager, to study and practice medicine in Africa.

From 1962-1964, he participated in the Epidemic Intelligence Service (EIS) of the Communicable Disease Center (CDC). Whilst at EIS, he became more interested in pursuing global health and spent a short time with the Peace Corps in India under Charles Snead Houston. Foege later entered the Master of Public Health program at the Harvard School of Public Health where he obtained his M.P.H. in 1965.

William Foege is a committed member of the Lutheran Church and admits to the influence of his Christian faith in his contribution to humanity.

Contribution to nation-building

William Foege's exceptional contributions to nation-building are numerous in the area of healthcare and they range from his efforts in the eradication of smallpox, in the treatment of river blindness to his contribution to the significant increase in child immunization. But the most prominent is his creative strategy that led to the successful eradication of smallpox. This was noted to be one of the most ambitious and most outstanding public health efforts of the 20th century.

Eradication of Smallpox

After earning a master's degree in public health from Harvard in 1965, he fulfilled his boyhood dream by volunteering to serve as a doctor for a hospital operated by the Lutheran Church in Yahe, Cross River State (now the Lutheran Hospital, Yahe).

In 1966, Dr. William Foege was asked to investigate reports of smallpox in a remote area of eastern Nigeria as part of the smallpox eradication effort of the U.S. Centers for Disease Control and Prevention in Nigeria. When he and his colleagues arrived, they found an outbreak raging. They didn't have enough vaccine for the standard response of mass inoculations and didn't have enough time to go back for more vacine. They had to come up with an alternative. "We asked ourselves: If we were smallpox viruses bent on immortality, what would we do next?" Foege recalled .

They decided to fight the epidemic by first identifying all known cases and then figuring out the most likely routes of further transmission based on family relationships, transportation patterns and commerce. They got out maps and radioed other missionaries in the area, asking them to get runners to every village to identify smallpox cases and report back. "Within 24 hours, we were able to pinpoint exactly where the smallpox was," Foege said. The group then set out with vaccine to immunize only those living in the three most likely "hot zones." It was a risky approach, but it worked. "Using only a small amount of vaccine, we stopped the outbreak,".

With this find-and-contain through ring immunization, interrupting the chain of transmission strategy of smallpox eradication, Foege created human shields against the spread of smallpox. This selective targeting approach he pioneered to end the smallpox outbreak was a success and the strategy, ultimately adopted globally, is credited with leading to the only successful global disease eradication campaign in history.

In 1973, he went to India to lead the smallpox battle there as thousands of people were dying from the disease. Indian health officials were reluctant to try anything other than mass vaccination (rejecting his targeted approach) but after intervention by an Indian physician, Foege was given a month to show he could contain the epidemic. He and his colleagues sent people from house-to-house to identify cases, with health care workers following later to vaccinate and were able to contain the outbreak. "In a year, India went from a country with the highest rate of smallpox to zero cases," he noted. In 1979, the World Health Organization declared smallpox eradicated — the first and, so far, only disease ever eliminated by deliberate public health action.

Because of his success in the smallpox campaign, Foege was

made director of CDC. He served as America's top disease detective from 1977 to 1983. The contribution of Dr Donald Henderson as head of the World Health Organisation smallpox eradication, in the global eradication of this killer disease, must also be lauded.

Child Immunisation

Dr Foege's other significant contribution to nation-building, is in the area of immunization. In 1978, the WHO member states committed themselves to immunizing 80% of the world's children, against a range of childhood diseases, by 1990, a huge increase from a starting rate of about 5 percent. By the mid-1980s, immunization rates were still only about 20 percent, so in 1984, WHO and other organizations called on Foege (then Professor of International Health at Emory University in Atlanta). As director of the Task Force for Child Survival and Development, Foege created a model for collaboration that has been replicated for other global health problems. By keeping the focus on the problem instead of turf wars, he played a central role in boosting immunization rates against the six basic diseases, in the developing world, to 80% within six years. James Grant, then the director of UNICEF, the United Nations Children's Fund, called the effort "the largest peacetime mobilization in the history of the Earth."

Treatment of River Blindness

In 1987, Merck & Co. found that a drug used to treat heartworm in dogs was effective in treating river blindness, then such a serious problem in Africa that in many villages most men over 40 were blind. At Foege's urging, Merck pledged to supply a form of the drug, Ivermectin, at no charge. But the company would do so only if the task force oversaw distribution. Suspicious of the industry, many of Foege's colleagues advised him to reject the conditions. But Foege had his mind on the victims. He took responsibility for the distribution, and what developed was arguably the first venture into pharmaco-philanthropy. One of the most effective public-private partnerships in global health, it virtually eradicated river blindness. Since then, other such partnerships have tackled drug-resistant tuberculosis, lymphatic filariasis, trachoma, and guinea worm.

He [Foege] is a member of the scientific board that helped design and implement the Grand Challenges in Global Health initiative, funded largely by the Gates Foundation. "The Grand Challenges program is looking at the problems that poor people face that aren't being addressed by the U.N. or other agencies," he explains. He has also been instrumental in child survival efforts, HIV/AIDS prevention, and the current quest to eradicate polio.

Dr William Foege is a man of faith who believes in a world where children can be protected from killer disease like diphtheria, tetanus, polio, measles, and whooping cough. He engineered the eradication of small pox, so we can believe the possibility of his dream and maybe our medical professionals can be inspired to pursue the eradication of our most common killer diseases such as Malaria, TB and Typhoid from our nation.

The Church

During this time I am thankful that I have been able, by the good hand of God upon me, to do something in mitigation of the miseries of this class, and to bring not only heavenly hopes and earthly gladness to the hearts of multitudes of these wretched crowds, but also many material blessings, including such commonplace things as food, raiment, home and work, the parent of so many other temporal benefits.

WILLIAM BOOTH

The story of the Salvation Army International cannot be separated from that of its founder William Booth. It was his vision that led to the founding of the church and it was still his vision that has enabled the church impact nations consistently for tens of decades now. Therefore, to discuss this case study, we will look at both William Booth and the church he founded, the Salvation Army International.

Background History

William Booth was born on the 10th of April 1829 in Sneinton, Nottingham, England and was the only son of four surviving children born to Samuel Booth and Mary Moss. He died on 20 August 1912 at the age of 83 years in Hadley Wood, London.

At the age of 13, his father went bankrupt and that pushed the family into poverty. To support his mother and sisters, he was apprenticed to a pawn-broker where he soon became fully aware of what poor people faced and how it causes their humiliation and degradation. During his teenage years he became a Christian and after his apprenticeship in 1848, he moved to London to work in the pawn broking trade. By 1852, he had trained himself in writing and in speech and became a fulltime Minister with the Methodist Church. He resigned from the Methodist Church in 1861.

According to the Salvation Army website, "In 1865, he and his wife Catherine opened The Christian Revival Society, was later renamed The Christian Mission, in the East End of London. In May 1878, Booth summoned his son, Bramwell, and his good friend, George Railton, to read a proof of the Christian Mission's annual report. At the top it read: THE CHRISTIAN MISSION is A VOLUNTEER ARMY. Bramwell strongly objected to this wording. He was not a volunteer: he was compelled to do God's work. So, in a flash of inspiration, Booth crossed out "Volunteer" and wrote "Salvation". The Salvation Army was born."

The Salvation Army was modelled after the military, with its own flag (or colours), uniform and "soldiers" with ranks. He became the "General" and his associates became "soldiers" with ranks given to ministers to reflect level of responsibility. Despite severe opposition, threat to their lives and even deaths, the 'General' and his 'officers' made and continues to make significant change in the nations of the world

The Wesley's Methodist legacy of commitment to both personal and social holiness (doctrine of sanctification and emphasis on social activism), the organizational genius of John Wesley and his own poverty experience, was a powerful influence in William Booth's life, theology and worldwide ministry.

His impact on the world was revealed when at his lying in state, 100,000 to 150,000 people showed up to pay tribute to the man who not only talked, but acted for the masses. The funeral was held at a vast exhibition hall on Hammersmith Road, in London drawing 40,000 people, including Queen Mary, who sat next to an ex-prostitute, a convert of General Booth's.

Contribution to nation-building

William Booth came on the scene when certain parts of England had a lot of people living in abject poverty in the midst of wealth. The government, the wealthy and even the church, did very little to address the plight of these people but complained about the rise in social vices (very much like Nigeria today).

Booth committed his life, despite the constant verbal and physical attacks, to not only focus on preaching salvation but also advocating and implementing social reforms. He was a man who believed that sometimes social improvement will come before conversion. He strongly believed that the role of the church was to: "loose the chains of injustice, free the captive and oppressed, share food and home, cloth the naked, and carry out family responsibilities." This was not an add-on service of the church but part of her calling and the Salvation Army was established as a vehicle for social reform alongside preaching the gospel.

Here are some of the contributions Booth and the Salvation Army made to nation-building.

Social Welfare

William Booth, his wife and associates, were involved in feeding the poor, through their "Food for the Million" shops (soup kitchens) and providing hostels for the homeless. The works of social compassion by the "Army" are legendary. Almost every type of outreach and care for the poor and downtrodden imaginable were attempted and usually successfully implemented. According to the Salvation Army website, "Today and across the world, The Salvation Army has 20 general hospitals, 45 maternity hospitals and 123 health centres/clinics, 440 hostels for homeless people, 228 children's homes, 116 homes for elderly people, 60 homes for disabled people, 12 homes for blind people, 57 remand and probation homes, 41 homes for street children, 41 mother and baby homes, 77 care homes for vulnerable people, 104 centres for people seeking refuge and 204 residential programmes for people with addiction dependency. The Salvation Army also has 2,286 education institutions which offer similar opportunities for ministry."

Through her Red Shield Services, The Salvation Army provides support services to the military, in Germany and UK only. This services ranges from non-alcoholic leisure facilities in military training establishments, to operating and managing children's groups and activities such as crèches, mothers and toddler groups, after school clubs in response to local need, to support families of military personnel left behind at base during wartime.

Disaster Relief

Since 1900 when she got involved in disaster relief efforts in the Galveston Hurricane in the US, The Salvation Army International has gone on to become one of the leading non-governmental relief agency and is usually among the first to arrive with help after natural or man-made disasters around the world. They work to alleviate suffering and help people rebuild their lives, including helping to retrieve and bury the dead, find survivors, rebuild homes, helping to re-establish the livelihood of the locals, supply drinking water, set up feeding units and kitchens and provide pastoral care to victims.

It must be noted that from the first and second world wars to the 2004, 2006 and 2011 tsunamis in Asia, to hurricanes in the US and the 9/11 terrorist attack, to drought and famine in Africa, small, medium and large scale relief work were carried out by her 'soldiers'.

Equal Rights

William Booth was deeply influenced by his wife Catherine because she was an inspired speaker, excellent in preparing sermons, she is reputed to have prepared many of his sermons, and a great supporter of his vision. As a result, William Booth gave women officer in the Salvation Army equal responsibility, with men, for preaching and social work. This was in a society that had not accepted women as equal to men (women were not even allowed to vote) and the result was attacks from the Church of England, politicians, and activist groups. Some attacks were not just verbal but physically, as members were violently attacked and imprisoned.

Booth and his wife were also active in the campaign to improve the working conditions of women. One of the famous examples is the Bryant and May case. A large number of the women working for Bryant and May factory (a match factory) in the East End of London suffered from 'Phossy Jaw' (necrosis of the bone), caused by the toxic fumes of yellow phosphorus from the matches, which eventually led to their deaths. Meanwhile the women were poorly paid. Booth suggested better alternatives to the company but these were rejected. To address this problem, the Salvation Army opened its own match-factory in Old Ford, East London in 1891, using the harmless red phosphorus. It also paid twice what Bryant and May paid their workers. He did not stop there but went further to conduct tours, for MPs and journalists, round the Salvation Army factory and the wretched homes of the Bryant and May workers. As a result of the bad publicity, the company stopped using the harmful yellow phosphorus. So, the 'Army' did not only stop the injustice against women but also used the opportunity to create jobs.

Advocacy

Advocacy is key part of Booth and the Army's contributions as they used their influence to lobby the Royal Family, politicians and other influential personalities. In his book, *In Darkest England and the Way Out*, Booth advocated applying the gospel and its ethics to the problems of crimes and poverty. He recommended establishing homes for the homeless; farm communities where the urban poor can be trained in agriculture; training and rehabilitation centers for prostitutes, released prisoners, drug addicts and alcoholics; financial aid for the poor; schemes for poor men's lawyers, banks, clinics, industrial schools; qualitative education for children and strong parenting in the family. He believed that if the state fails to meet its social obligations it will be the task of each Christian to step into the breach.

This book was a blueprint for the rehabilitation of an entire nation, a grand social reconstruction plan a century ahead of its time. What Booth suggested forms the foundation for the Salvation Army's modern social welfare schemes and had an impact in the establishment of the British Welfare System (including the National Health Service). Today, "The Salvation Army is one of the world's largest providers of social aid, with expenditures including operating costs of $2.6 billion in 2004, helping more than 32 million people in the US alone."

Civil Rights

I have a dream that one day on the red hills of Georgia, the sons of former slaves and the sons of former slave owners will be able to sit together at the table of brotherhood.

DR MARTIN LUTHER KING JNR

Background History

Martin Luther King, Jr., was born 15th January 1929, in Atlanta, Georgia. He was the first son and second child of Reverend Martin Luther King, Sr. and Alberta Williams King. Dr King attended Booker T. Washington High School. At the age of 15 he progressed to Morehouse College where he graduated in 1948 with a Bachelor of Arts degree in sociology. After graduation, King enrolled in Crozer Theological Seminary in Pennsylvania where he graduated in 1951 with a Bachelor of Divinity degree. With a fellowship won at Crozer, King began doctoral studies in systematic theology at Boston University and received a Doctor of Philosophy degree on the 5th of June 1955.

In 1954, King became pastor of the Dexter Avenue Baptist Church in Montgomery, Alabama when he was twenty-five years old. Always a advocate of civil rights for members of his race, King was, by this time, a member of the executive committee of the National Association for the Advancement of Colored People, the leading organization of its kind in the nation. In December 1955, King led the Montgomery Bus Boycott which was the first Negro nonviolent demonstration of contemporary times in the United States. The boycott lasted 382 days. During which, King was arrested, subjected to personal abuse, his home was bombed but he emerged as a Negro leader of the first rank. In his lifetime, King was arrested upwards of twenty times and assaulted at least four times. In 1957, King with Ralph Abernathy and other civil rights activists, of that time, founded the Southern Christian Leadership Conference (SCLC). The group was created to harness the moral authority and organizing power of black churches to conduct nonviolent protests for civil rights reform. King led the SCLC until his death. The ideals for this organization he took from Christianity but its operational techniques where from Gandhi.

There are two key personalities who inspired Dr King. The first was his father's classmate at Morehouse College, Howard Thurman. Thurman was a civil rights leader, theologian, and educator who mentored King during his student days. The second was Mahatma Gandhi who, incidentally, influenced Thurman as well. In 1959, King visited the Gandhi family in India and that trip affected King in a profound way, deepening his understanding of non-violent resistance and his commitment to America's civil rights struggle.

At the age of 35, Martin Luther King, Jr., was the youngest man to have received the Nobel Peace Prize for his work to end racial segregation and racial discrimination through civil disobedience and other nonviolent means. When notified of his selection, he announced that he would turn over the prize money of $54,123 for the furtherance of the civil rights movement. He is frequently referenced as a human rights icon globally and has inspired many more civil right movements around the world (including movements in South Africa).

There are very few individuals whose name, speeches and legacy have often been invoked as Dr Martin Luther King, Jnr. On the evening of 4th April 1968, while standing on the balcony of his motel room in Memphis, Tennessee, where he was to lead a protest march in sympathy with striking garbage workers of that city, he was assassinated. He died at the age of 39. He was posthumously awarded the Presidential Medal of Freedom in 1977 and Congressional Gold Medal in 2004. Martin Luther King, Jr. Day was declared a US national holiday in 1986.

Contribution to nation-building

Racial Equality

From an early age, Dr King witnessed racial segregation against African Americans and was determined to do all he could to change the way America treated African Americans. There were three key tools which contributed to Dr King's success, namely:

> 1. extraordinary oratory (a great speaker with ability to demand attention and action with his words)
> 2. exceptional ability to effectively mobilise and organise a crowd to action
> 3. Nonviolent approach to protest.

These were what he used to accelerate the fight against inequality.

Oratory: Efforts had been made in the past by minorities groups to fight the inequality in America but it was during Dr King's leadership that these efforts were taken to a whole new level. A primary reason for this was Dr King's exceptional oratory skills and this helped in a big way to galvanize support for protest campaigns by African Americans and white Americans.

His ability to demand attention and instigate action, not only helped forge unity amongst the various black civil rights leaders and organisations but also contributed to destroying the myth of inferiority of black people held by many white Americans. In 1963, he gave the famous 'I have a dream ... " speech in front of over 250,000 people, then the largest crowd of protesters in the history of Washington DC, and that speech is widely recognized as one of the best speeches ever given. Not only because of its content and delivery but also because of the change it inspires in America and around the world. For many in the US, and around the world, Barack Obama's presidency is a fulfilment of the desires expressed in that speech.

Mobilisation: With the organised mobilisation of African Americans in the South and support from some white

Americans, Dr King led numerous protest campaigns. These campaigns all culminated in the abortion of racial segregation laws. The first of those campaigns that brought Dr King national recognition, was the Montgomery Bus Boycott of 1955. On December 1955, Rosa Park refused to obey the Jim Crow segregation law which required her to give up her seat in the bus for a white man. This resulted in the driver calling the police and she was arrested. There had been few instances of this sort of civil disobedience but on this occasion, Dr King with some associates responded to Rosa Park's arrest by extensively organising and mobilising the boycott of the Montgomery public transit system.

African Americans, the main customers of the Montgomery public transit, boycott the buses and choose to trek everywhere, to work, school, place of worship, etc., share private cars with fellow blacks or use organised discounted black cab or cycled. The result was financial distress for the public transit system from loss of patronage. Despite physical attacks, arrests, convictions with jail terms, Dr King and black Americans persisted with the boycott, until the Supreme Court upheld the ruling of a district court to the effect that Alabama and Montgomery laws requiring segregated buses were unconstitutional. That meant, African Americans were allowed to sit anywhere in the bus and did not have to give up their seats to white Americans.

With that Supreme Court ruling, the boycott was officially brought to an end on the 20th of December 1956 after 381 days. The impact of this well mobilised and organised protest was not limited to the ruling against racial segregation but it inspired further campaigns against all other existing areas of segregation in the American society.

Other campaigns were organised and led by Dr King and SCLC, joining with other civil rights movements to fight for other rights i.e., voting rights, labour rights, jobs and better pay for blacks and poor whites, appropriate civil rights legislations and an end to racial segregation in all facets of the society. These campaigns includes the Alabama Movement of 1961, the Birmingham Campaign of 1963, the St Augustine Florida Campaign of 1964, Selma Alabama Campaign of 1964 and 1965 and Chicago Campaign of 1966.

Nonviolent Approach: With the significant media coverage, the nonviolent nature of most of these campaigns drew public sympathy and support from the white American public, most of whom could no longer tolerate the arrest, torture and other inhuman treatment meted to nonviolent protesters by the police and other government agencies. All these culminated in the passage into law of the Civil Rights Act of 1964 and the Voting Rights Act of 1965.

The impact of nonviolent protest campaigns on nation-building in America (like in India where Gandhi had earlier practiced nonviolent civil disobedience) cannot be over emphasised. America may still have cases of racial discrimination but it is now a society where African Americans are able to study in whatever field of endeavour and at any institution, choose where they live, who they vote for and even become President.

National Integration

Prior to the 60s, most whites in America were prejudiced against blacks, largely, due to ignorance which was a result of minimal contact with other races and negative influence and traditions passed down by their ancestors. Dr King's persistent fight against racial segregation with his gift of oratory, organising and mobilising ability, nonviolent protests and the extensive media coverage, made many whites begin to accept that the ridiculous practice of segregation and unequal treatment of blacks, was not the dream of the American founders, nor was it supported by biblical scripture. The result was that many whites changed their perception of blacks, developed friendship with African Americans and other minorities and in fact, a few joined in the fight against racial segregation. The product was a more tolerant nation.

Dr King and SCLC launched the Poor Peoples Campaign in 1967 to fight poverty. This movement shifted focus from civil right to the fight against economic injustice, in American, which was a product of long years of segregation. Using peaceful marches, lobbying and speeches, this campaign fought for the provision of decent housing, better education and more job opportunities and training for African Americans, other minorities and white Americans. It was during this phase of the battle that he was assassinated. Dr King did not see his campaign as a fight for blacks only, but primarily as a fight for a better America in line with the vision of her founders. A nation that is prosperous with proper distribution of wealth and protects equally, the rights and opportunities for its diverse people.

Politics

If we say that we believe in democracy, if we say that the fabric of a democratic society is one which allows for the free play of idea ... then, in the name of all the gods, give that free play a chance to work within the constitutional framework.

LEE KUAN YEW

Background History

Lee Kuan Yew was born 16th September 1923 to Lee Chin Koon and Chua Jim Neo. With a strong British cultural influence on his family, he was given the name Harry by his grandfather. Lee studied at Telok Kurau Primary School, Raffles Institution, and Raffles College in Singapore. After the Second World War, he moved to England where he spent a brief time at the London School of Economics before moving to Cambridge University, to study law. On the 1st of August 1950, he returned to Singapore and joined the law practice of Laycock and Ong. This was the legal practice of John Laycock, a British pioneer of multiracialism in Singapore and one of the founders of the Singapore Progressive Party, which Lee joined as an election agent for John. He later left to establish his own legal practice, Lee and Lee, with his wife and elder brother.

Because the Singapore Progressive Party was made up of English speaking upper class professionals, Lee left the party to form a broader based party. On the 12th of November 1954, Lee with some associates formed the People's Action Party (PAP) which had alliance with the Chinese working class. It was on the platform of this party that he contested a seat in parliament during the 1955 elections and became the opposition leader against the David Marshall's Labour Front led coalition government. He was also one of PAP's representatives to the two constitutional discussions held in London over the future status of Singapore. With the PAP winning 43 out of the 51 seats in the legislative assembly at the 1959 national elections, Lee became the first Prime Minister of self governed Singapore on the 5th of June 1959.

After independence from the British and as part of Lee's effort to ensure the survival of Singapore, he accepted a proposal from the Malayan Prime Minister Tunku Abdul Rahman to merge with Malaysia. On 16th September 1963, the Federation of Malaysia was formed. Due to ethnic, religious and ideological differences, the merger failed despites all efforts by Lee to resolve the differences. On the 9th of August 1965 the Malaysian Parliament passed the resolution that severed Singapore's ties to Malaysia as a state, that same day the Republic of Singapore was created.

This new independent nation was faced with numerous problems which were compounded by the failed merger with Malaysia. She lacked natural resources, very limited defensive capabilities, no independent water supply, insufficient educational and housing infrastructures, a very high unemployment rate and a potentially explosive multi-racial society. These are the challenges that faced Lee and his PAP led government. It begged for a visionary leadership to build her into a great nation and that is what Lee and his government provided.

Contribution to nation-building

I believe, Lee's greatest contribution to nation-building was in providing visionary leadership to: an infant nation facing desperate times, after independence; a developing nation faced with challenges on which direction to take; and to a developed nation that seeks to sustain her prosperity for generations to come.

Amongst his numerous contributions to nation-building, 2 key areas stand out – Economic and Social contribution.

Economic Contribution

The combined factors of the failed merger with Malaysia, with potential common market and expanded domestic market and the withdrawal of the significant British military presence from Singapore with heavy job losses, left Lee with a nation in desperate economic woes by the time she was declared a republic in 1965. Lee recognized that Singapore needed a strong economy in order to survive as an independent country, and with a small domestic market, he launched a programme to industrialised Singapore by transforming her into a major finished-goods exporter.

In 1967, the Economic Development Board was established to attract foreign investment, offering them attractive tax incentives and providing access to the highly skilled, disciplined and relatively low-paid work force. The board offered financial incentives to attract export industries, promote trade and end the country's dependence on Britain as the major source of investment capital. With a buoyant world economic in the 60s, Singapore became a supply centre for the United States in its increasing involvement in Indochina and also resumed trade relations with Indonesia and Japan. These partnerships accelerated the development and growth of the Singapore economy.

To encourage and sustain this growth, Lee's government

ensured tight regulatory control of the capital resources, labour (through labour laws), family planning and land allocation. The result of these controls was stability of the economy, diverse businesses and manufacturers, better labour relations between employers and labour unions, better training and productivity and recruitment of Singaporeans with good remuneration. It must be added that Lee's government move swiftly to provide the infrastructure needed to support this rapid growth. They provided first class airports, ports, roads, communications network, industrial estates, schools, health care and public services. The government took advantage of the British pullout to convert some of the military facilities for commercial and industrial purposes and re-trained the over 21,000 laid-off workers for new jobs. An example of this is the former King George VI Graving Dock which was converted to the Sembawang Shipyard, employing 3,000 former naval base workers in ship building and ship repair. By 1975 Singapore was the world's third busiest port after Rotterdam and New York and the container trans-shipment centre of southeast Asia.

Having seen the transformation of Singapore into an investors haven, major multinationals from United States, Western Europe, Japan, Hong Kong, Taiwan, Malaysia and Australia moved in to set up major operations in the country. By 1972, United States firms accounted for 46% of new foreign capital invested in Singapore. Also by the early 1970s, Singapore not only had nearly full employment but also faced labour shortages in some areas. As a result, immigration laws and work permit requirements were relaxed and by 1972 immigrant workers made up 12 percent of the labour force.

Even without a domestic oil reserves (though her neighbours are oil rich), her stability, regulatory controls, first class infrastructure and the reliability and quality of her labour market, has made Singapore the third largest oil refining centre in the world. Today, Singapore is one of the wealthiest countries in the world with one of the world's highest per capita incomes, huge foreign reserve and no foreign debt.

Social Contribution

To enable Singapore become and remain an investors haven, Lee visionary leadership manifested in key social initiatives. These initiatives not only provided the skilled workforce required but also significantly improved the quality of life of Singaporeans.

Housing: This was one of the primary areas of concern when Singapore gained independence. Lee established the Housing and Development Board (HDB) to tackle the problem. Within 5 years, over 54,000 housing unit had been built and rented out to low income earners, most of whom previously lived in squatter settlements. Also, schemes were introduced for these people to buy their flats instead of renting them. To Lee, his housing policies were not just to provide shelter for his people but also a means to promote social cohesion (through quota system), improve quality of life, pride of house ownership and an incentive to work hard. Today, about 90% of the people in Singapore live in HDB flats.

Education: At independence, Singapore had a high number of people without formal education resulting in high unemployment rate. Therefore, Lee viewed education as a tool to address the unemployment problem. He invested heavily, about one fifth of her budget, in education to produce the skilled workforce that would make Singapore attractive to investor, who are to provide employment. The intensive educational system was based on the English language (as that would be the language of the expatriates) and focused more on practical subjects like technical sciences than on the intellectual subjects like philosophy. The result of this heavy investment and strategy has produced a nation with a well educated and highly skilled workforce who are gainfully employed and well paid. It also helps to sustain the nation as an investment destination. Today, Singapore is the base for top class institutions like the Colombo Plan Staff College for Technical Education, the Regional Institure of Higher Education and Development (RIHED) and the Regional Language Center (RELC).

Savings Scheme (Central Provident Fund): This saving scheme was set up by the colonial government, but Lee's government changed its focus from just a simple retirement scheme to a fund that also enabled Singaporeans to buy their homes, pay for Medi-care, buy shares in multinational companies in their country, and so on. This is one of the few nations in the world where most of her citizens have a scheme that meets their essential needs for food, shelter, healthcare, etc. Through this policy, Lee ensured that Singaporeans benefitted immensely from the wealth created in their country.

National Identity: Through the Constitutional Commission on Minority Rights established in 1965, Lee's government proactively sought to integrate her diverse ethnic groups and create a Singaporean identity. This deliberate government policy was implemented through schools and the public housing schemes.

Discipline: Lee's government also proactively sought to emphasis discipline and the need for a strong work ethic by communicating to the people the nation's bid to become self reliant and prosperous. He supported this by promptly and firmly dealing with any acts of indiscipline (including corruption) at all levels of his government. It is generally believed that Lee's anti corruption stands is one of his key legacies and a key reason why he has been able to accelerate and sustain the development of Singapore. Lee is known to be a man of integrity and through his visionary leadership he created a nation that moved from ethnic conflicts, crime and indiscipline to a nation with high work ethics, prudent people, disciplined and orderly people, very low corruption rate and a melting pot of Chinese, Malaysian, Indian and Arabic communities.

Lee Kuan Yew visionary leadership achieved enormous successful because his vision for Singapore, transformed into policies, were well thought out, rigorously implemented and single-mindedly enforced. His style bordered on authoritarianism but such was the level of integrity, discipline and focus he had and also demanded from his associates and every Singaporeans. The end product was the transformation of the third world mosquito-infested swamp full of poor people into a first world vibrant developed nation of prosperous people, in one generation.

It must be noted that for all Lee's success, very little would have been achieved if the Singaporeans were not active players in his efforts. They put in long hours at work, gave up a lot of labour rights, initially earned less than the hours put in, and so on. In summary, they shared the fears of their leaders about the security of their nation and the government's vision of what was required for a prosperous and independent Singapore. They willingly gave up their comfort to make these sacrifices and put in enormous hard work to achieve the hard task set by Lee's administration. It is these qualities of the typical Singaporean that provided the platform for Lee's government success.

Social Entrepreneurship

People can change their own lives, provided they have the right kind of institutional support. They're not asking for charity, charity is no solution to poverty. [Microcredit] is the creation of opportunities like everybody else has, not the poor people, so bring them to the poor people, so that they can change their lives.

MUHAMMAD YUNUS

Background History

Muhammad Yunus, known as the "Banker to the Poor", was born 28th June 1940 in Chittagong in the south-eastern region of Bangladesh, the third of nine children. His education started in his village primary school and continued at Lamabazar Primary School and Chittagong Collegiate School. After which he studied at Chittagong College and in 1957, he entered Dhaka University where he got his first degree in 1960 and masters in 1961, both in economics. In 1969, he obtained his Ph.D in the same discipline from the Vanderbilt University in the United States of America.

Yunus began as a lecturer at the Chittagong College and went on to lecture at the Middle Tennessee State University in the US. After the liberation war of Bangladesh, Yunus returned home in 1972 and worked briefly for the government planning commission but returned to the teaching profession where he became the Head of the Economics Department at the Chittagong University. By 1975, Yunus was a Professor of Economics.

In 1974, Yunus confronted with the severe famine that hit Bangladesh and led to the death of thousands abandoned the economic theories he had learnt in university and sought out a solution that was relevant to the problems of his people. These search culminated in the creation of the "Grameen Bank",. inspired by Dr. Akhtar Hameed Khan, who is credited with pioneering the concept of providing credit to the poor as a tool for poverty alleviation.

Contribution to nation-building

Poverty Alleviation

The main contribution of Yunus to nation-building is in the area of poverty alleviation. His reaction to the devastating famine that hit Bangladesh in 1974 produced programmes that, many years after, have improved the quality of life of the people, many of whom would probably not be alive today but for the programmes. According to Yunus, poverty in Bangladesh decreased by 1% per year till 2000 and by 2% till 2005 (statistics beyond 2005 is not yet available). He believes that where this rate is sustained, poverty level could decrease by 50% by 2015 and possibly be eradicated by 2030. We can not fault his enthusiasm especially when you consider that Bangladesh is one of the poorest countries in the world and any reversal of the poverty trend will be greatly appreciated, particularly, in an era when rich nations are seeing an increase in their poverty level.

These programmes later came under the umbrella of the Grameen Bank. Let's look at the specifics of his contributions to poverty alleviation:

Microcredit Schemes: Confronted with a situation where the majority of his people were poor, unemployed with no credit facilities to enable or support income generation, Yunus' vision was to see the availability of microcredit as a vehicle to provide these poor people with a means of livelihood. He started by providing loans from his own pocket to women who produced bamboo furniture and with the success of this scheme on a small scale, he persuaded the government owned Janata Bank to provide the microcredit schemes. With the support of Janata Bank, Yunus was able to significantly increase the number of beneficiaries of the microcredit. By 1982, the scheme had over 28,000 members. This success led to the establishment of Grameen Bank in 1983. It is important to note that beneficiaries of this scheme were people with no money, no collaterals, the poorest of the society with no evidence of their ability to pay back the loans. But Yunus believed that these impoverished people had skills and abilities that were under-utilized and only the availability of funds would result in the expression of such skills and abilities and improve their standard of living.

Yunus commented:

Their poverty was not a personal problem due to laziness or lack of intelligence, but a structural one: lack of capital. Besides, some money-lenders set interest rates as high as 10 per cent a month, some 10 per cent a week! The existing system made it certain that however hard the poor worked, they would never raise themselves above subsistence level. What was needed was to link their work to capital to allow them to amass an economic cushion and earn a ready income.

He further noted that:

Poverty covers people in a thick crust and makes the poor appear stupid and without initiative. Yet if you give them credit, they will slowly come back to life. Even those who seemingly have no conceptual thought, no ability to think of yesterday or tomorrow, are in fact quite intelligent and an expert at the art of survival. Credit is the key that unlocks their humanity.

Since the inception of the Microcredit scheme, over $8 billion microcredit has been made available and today, it is making a difference in the lives of nearly 8 million of its beneficiaries, over 40 million when you include family members, in Bangladesh and millions more in other countries (including developed nations) who have replicated this model. The microcredit scheme from Grameen bank impacts upon the lives of nearly a third of the Bangladesh population, directly or indirectly, becoming one of the key vehicles for building that nation. Note that contrary to the view held by commercial banks, majority of the members paid back their loans and this they do to ensure the continuous availability of the facility, social responsibility to fellow members and to enable them qualify for bigger facilities.

Women Empowerment: Yunus is a firm believer that a nation can only fully develop when the women are empowered. Today, about 94% of the Grameen Bank schemes beneficiaries are women. Like in many poor countries, the women in Bangladesh fared worse than the men. They received little education, were married off early, were abandoned or divorced by their husbands especially when he marries a new wife, not given job opportunities, essentially, they were and still are considered of little value and treated as second class citizens and conventionally, banks lend mainly to men. On many occasions, when abandoned, divorced or widowed, they were left to fend for the children. Hence, women and their children are the poorest of the poor in a developing nation like Bangladesh.

Yunus viewed this attitude as a key contributor to a nation's inability to become developed especially since he believed women are better money managers, are more responsible and accountable when given loans and more industrious. He therefore set out to alleviate their poverty by making women the core target of his microcredit schemes. His first client was a woman named Sufia Khatun who made bamboo furniture in Jobra, the village next to his campus. Due to lack of funds to buy raw materials, this woman was forced to borrow from a moneylender and the payment term was that she sells the finished product to him at a price fixed by him. The price fixed by the moneylender meant she made a profit of only 2 cents a day. Yunus put together a group of people with similar challenges and granted them loans from his pocket. They used the money to pay off the moneylenders, buy raw materials and sold the finished products to the highest bidder. Instead of the previous profit of 2 cent a day, Sufia was able to make $1.25 a day. This enabled her increase her borrowing, make more products and increase sales, which resulted in bigger profits. This is a typical story for most of the women who are beneficiaries of the Grameen bank schemes. Yunus vision is proven right in the fact that Grameen bank achieves almost 99% loan repayment rate despite most of these women joining the scheme as beggars, destitute, illiterates, divorcees, widows, etc.

This economic empowerment gave the women income to educate their children, expand their trade, open savings accounts for their children's training and future security and feed the family including their husband. In addition, these women now have a sense of worth to create community where they support one another to utilise their skills and abilities. Many of these women have improved the standard of living of their families and there are studies that indicate that the success these women achieve has led to respect from their husbands, respect from men generally, reduced divorce and birth rates in the community. This illustrates the multiple effects of women empowerment as a means for poverty alleviation.

Social Business Enterprise: Yunus saw the poor as bankable which is a radical change from normal banking approach. He viewed banking as a social business and as a result, Grameen Bank became a full-fledged bank, in 1983, to provide loans to poor Bangladeshis with no collateral. His bank model operates with corporate efficiency and focus on social efforts by pumping profits back into social objectives. Today, with 2,500 branches in Bangladesh covering three quarters of the rural areas of the country, Grameen Bank has provided over $8 billion loans to over 7 million borrowers in Bangladesh. Independent studies by World Bank and others indicate that within five years, about half Grameen's borrowers manage to pull themselves out of poverty, while a further quarter hover near the poverty line.

Its system is largely based on mutual trust and the enterprise and accountability of her borrowers (or members) For example, to ensure repayment, the bank uses a system of small groups applying for loans together and its members act as co-guarantors for repayment and support one another's efforts at economic self-advancement.

Also, the bank officials and the members (borrowers) are bound by set principles and commitments which they also impart to new members. The objective of these personal commitments, known as the "16 decisions", is to ensure that members are focused on not just making profits but also maintaining healthy, disciplined lives and work ethics, which will enable them sustain their improved quality of life and allow others benefit from them. To be eligible for a Grameen Bank loan, a member has to be committed to these personal commitments and principles, while current members are also encouraged to maintain their dedication to the "16 decisions". This is another way Grameen Bank highlights her focus as a social business that does not just provide loans for the poor but is actively seeking to improve and sustain both the economic and social aspects of the Bangladesh nation.

Yunus was once asked how to reform a business to have a larger social impact. He remarked that the first step was reconsidering what constitutes social help. He said, "Charity money only has one life, [...] It goes out, does the job and never comes back. But if you convert it into a social business, it becomes a very powerful business because the money is recycled." A good illustration is the fact that the borrowers own 92 per cent of the bank shares and the balance is owned by the Bangladesh government. So, the bank is not only a bank for the poor but also by the poor.

Still focused on her objectives as a social business, Grameen Bank has expanded into new initiatives in profit and non-profit ventures which includes Grameen Fisheries Foundation, Grameen Agriculture Foundation, Grameen Trust, Grameen Fund (equity investors in several SME businesses including Grameen Software, Grameen CyberNet, Grameen Knitwear), and Grameen Telecom which has a stake in the biggest private sector phone company in Bangladesh, Grameenphone (GP). GP is behind the Vilage Phone (Polli Phone) project that has so far enabled over 260,000 poor Bangladeshis to own affordable GSM phones as profit making venture. The success of Yunus social business concept has attracted interest from several blue chip companies keen to create non-profit/non-loss businesses with the sole aim of ploughing back all the profits into the business to improving people's lives by offering affordable and much desired products and part ownership. A Grameen partnership with Danone was established to address the problem of malnutrition of millions of children in Bangladesh. The objective of this partnership was to produce yogurt with added micronutrients at affordable prices to help improve the health of children. They also partnered with BASF to produce chemically treated mosquito-nets to curb malaria and with

Intel to bring affordable information technology solutions to rural villages.

Muhammad Yunus exceptional contribution to nation-building has earned him numerous awards globally and that includes the 2006 Nobel Peace Prize, jointly with Grameen Bank. He used his share of the $1.4 million award money to create a company to make low-cost, high-nutrition food and also to set up an eye hospital for the poor. Today, more than 250 institutions in nearly 100 countries operate microcredit programs and social business initiatives based on the Grameen Bank model, while thousands of other microcredit programs have emulated, adapted or been inspired by the Grameen Bank. According to an expert on innovative government, the program established by Yunus at the Grameen Bank "is the single most important development in the third world in the last 100 years, and I don't think any two people will disagree."

Summary

The common theme for each of these nation-builders is that their thoughts, words and actions were all geared towards identifying a problem and seeking solutions — study phase, implementing actions — practice and teaching phase and in the process, inspiring others to do same —inspire phase. Note that the core nation-building values of Compassion, Opportunity, Responsibility, Equality, Valour, Ambition, Liberty, Unity, Enterprise and Spirituality were at work to transform and focus their thoughts, words and actions. I hope, like me, you were inspired by reading each brief case study.

Does Nigeria have nation-builders? Most certainly! We have had people like Gani Fawehinmi, Prof. Ransome-Kuti, Tai Solarin and several others but when we consider the size of our population we would agree that we have, by far, too few nation-builders. Nigerians, therefore, need to gain further inspiration from efforts of ordinary individuals from other nations to enable us arise and build our nation today.

Conclusion

*What this country needs is more people to inspire
others with confidence, and fewer people to discourage
any initiative in the right direction; more to get into the
thick of things, fewer to sit on the sidelines, merely
finding fault; more to point out what's right with the
world, and fewer to keep harping on what's wrong
with it and more who are interested in lighting candles,
and fewer who blow them out.*
FATHER JAMES KELLER

In his book, *Epic of America*, James Truslow Adams coined the
phrase the American dream and described it thus:

> The American Dream is that dream of a land in
> which life should be better and richer and fuller
> for every man, with opportunity for each
> according to ability or achievement. It is a
> difficult dream for the European upper classes to
> interpret adequately, also too many of us have
> grown weary and mistrustful of it. It is not a
> dream of motor cars and high wages merely, but
> a dream of social order in which each man and
> each woman shall be able to attain to the fullest
> stature of which they are innately capable, and be
> recognized by others for what they are, regardless
> of the fortuitous circumstances of birth or
> position.

He explained that:

> The American Dream that has lured tens of
> millions of all nations to our shores in the past
> century has not been a dream of material plenty,
> though that has doubtlessly counted heavily. It
> has been a dream of being able to grow to fullest

development as a man and woman, unhampered
by the barriers which had slowly been erected in
the older civilizations, unrepressed by social
orders which had developed for the benefit of
classes rather than for the simple human being of
any and every class.

From the above, we can deduce that the summary of the
American Dream is the freedom of every citizen of the
country to be all they can be to the benefit of the individual
and the nation. The vision of that nation remains the vision
of the typical American, including the immigrants who have
made America their home, and it is pursued vigorously in
their daily lives, thereby influencing their thoughts, words
and actions. We would agree that America is not a perfect
nation, by any means, but we can not dispute the fact that this
country provides opportunities for everybody to be all they are
ordained by God to be — when they give it their best shot. The
world biggest economy and superpower, is really a land of
opportunities. I strongly believe that Nigeria has the same
potential to become as great as America. But to achieve this,
we must have a Nigerian Dream, one that every citizen must
value, practice, teach and inspire in others. We have to be a
nation (a people) that has a vision and pursues that vision in
all sphere of life.

In my view, the Nigerian Dream should mean a nation where
we believe in and pursue the nation-building core values. It
is in the pursuit of these values that we would produce a land
of opportunities for all within the confines of responsibility
and spirituality. A nation where all Nigerians are treated as
equals and given the platform to be all they can be, regardless
of their status, educational background, ethnic group,
profession, religion, etc.

This Nigerian Dream is one where we not only practise and
live these values but also demand them from other Nigerians
by what we teach and inspire. In effect, our goal should be to
have a transformed mindset, words and actions and to also

proactively seek to replicate this in the lives of people in our circle of influence. But it must be reiterated that the best way to influence is practice. We have to become a country of integrity that says do as I do and not only do as I say. As Bill Halamandaris stated, "Values are not hereditary. Great ideals do not live in the minds of men simply because they are right. They must be taught. They must be learned and lived."

I expect that having read this book you would:

- agree that nation-building holds the key to the transformation of our nation from its current state of crisis to a developed nation that provides a guarantee of a better life for our children and for African nations.
- appreciate fully the reasons why we must build our nation, knowing that this provides the motivation to accept the core values required.
- accept and defend the core values that will transform our mindset, our words and our actions. This will result in a changed lifestyle for us and for people around us.
- act on the steps involved in implementing nation-building, in general and in specific areas unique to our capacities, abilities, talents, experience and callings, on a daily basis.
- accept the family as the primary platform for the study, practice, teaching and inspiring of nation-building using the unique roles of fathers and mothers.
- acknowledge the unique role that churches and mosques can and must play in mobilizing her members to become nation-builders by prioritizing the nation in her activities. There must also be a demand by members on the leadership to focus on the nation.
- finally, be inspired to arise and change the nation just like many ordinary people in history have done.

Martin Luther King, Jr. once stated, "Human progress is neither automatic nor inevitable .... Every step toward the goal of justice requires sacrifice, suffering, and struggle; the tireless exertions and passionate concern of dedicated individuals." Building a nation is neither automatic nor inevitable, we are required to lay down our lives to achieve the Nigerian Dream. John F. Kennedy said, "There are risks and costs to a program of action, but they are far less than the long range risks and costs of comfortable inaction."

Now is the time for Nigerians to rise up with courage and build this nation, irrespective of the cost to us but anticipating the benefits to the nation in our lifetime and our children's. The bible says, "The point is this: whoever sows sparingly will also reap sparingly, and whoever sows bountifully will also reap bountifully." It is time to sow bountifully.

It is time to arise and build!

Personal Worksheet
How To Implement Nation-Building

Responsibility: How can I accept responsibility for Nigeria?

Review: What values are my strengths and which ones do I need to improve upon?

Identification: What am I good at doing?
What do I love to do?
What need must I serve?
How can I align my talent with my passion in order to meet the need that burdens me?

Planning: What is my plan of action to implement what I have identified?
What assistance do I need?
When do I intend to implement?

Practice

Initiative: What actions have I taken to implement my plan?

Momentum: What am I doing to sustain and accelerate my efforts?

Teach

Communication: What do my family and friend say about what I communicate and how do I improve?

Modelling: Who is my role model and who am I modelling to?
What am I modelling in my family, workplace and community?

Mentoring: Who am I mentoring? Is there anyone else I can mentor?

Inspire

Who inspires me and why?
How do I inspire others like I have been inspired?

The Nation-Builder's Pledge

I pledge to put Nigeria first in my thoughts, words and actions

I pledge to apply the core values in my daily life

I pledge to study, practice, teach and inspire nation-building in my life and in my circle of influence

I pledge to use my family and my faith as a platform for nation-building

I pledge to join at least one nation-building group and create a group in an area without an existing group

Select Bibliography

"Americans give record $295B to charity". USA Today, 25 June 2007.

ADAMS, JAMES TRUSLOW. The Epic of America. (1931).

BACH, RICHARD. Running from Safety: An Adventure of the Spirit (1994).

BEEBE, STEVEN et al. Interpersonal Communication: Relating to Others. (2007).

BLAIR, TONY. "Final Press Conference at the end of the 2005 G8 Summit in Gleneagles". (2005).

BONHOEFFER, DIETRICH. Letters and Papers from Prison (1943-1945). (1967).

BOYD, JAMES W. "Godly Motherhood", O, Give Me A Home (Chapter 9; e-book).

COLE, DELE. "Nigerian banks and the people". The Punch Newspaper, 26 February (2009).

COOLIDGE, CALVIN. President Coolidge's speech – 150th Anniversary of Phillips Academy, Andover. (1928).

COVEY, STEPHEN. The 4 Steps to Finding Your Voice. (2008).

DADA, KAMIL. "Yunus pushes microcredit" The Standard Daily, 17 November (2008).

DECKET, PAUL T. et al. The Effects of Teach for America on Students: Findings from a National Evaluation. (2004).

DISRAELI, BENJAMIN. Speech in the House of Commons. (1849).

DOBBINS, JAMES. Nation-Building: the Inescapable Responsibility of the World's Only Superpower. (RAND Review Summer 2003).

DORF, PHILIP. Liberty Hyde Bailey: An Informal Biography (LHB). (1956:78).

ESQUIVEL, LAURA. Swift as Desire. (2001).

GORDON, G. and EVANS, B. The mission of the church and the role of Advocacy. (2002:2).

GRACIAS, VALERIAN CARDINAL. The Role of Christian Colleges in Indian National Development. (1967:32).

HALAMANDARIS, BILL. The Heart of America: Ten Core Values That Make Our Country. (2004).

HAYEK, FRIEDRICH A. The Constitution of Liberty, University of Chicago Press. (1960).

HOOVER, HERBERT C. President's Inaugural Address. (1929).

JEFFERSON, THOMAS. American Declaration of Independence. (1776).

JOLIS, ALAN. "The Good Banker", The Independent on Sunday Supplement, 5 May.

KOPP, WENDY. One Day, All Children ... : The Unlikely Triumph of Teach For America and What I Learned Along The Way. New York. Public Affairs, 2001. (2003).

MARDEN, ORISON SWETT. Pushing To The Front. (1911:13).

MAXWELL, JOHN. Momentum Breakers vs. Momentum Makers. (2009).

MAXWELL, JOHN. Principle-Centered Planning. (2009).

MOONEY, B and HOLT, D. The Storyteller's Guide. (1996:9).

NELSON, GAYLORD. (1970).

OBAMA, BARRACK. President's Inaugural Address. (USA, 2009).

Partnering to roll back malaria in Bauchi State. UNICEF Report, 22 April 2009.

PAULSON, TOM "A lifetime spent in the war on disease", Seattle Post Intelligencer Reporter, 22 March (2001).

PAYNE, JAMES. A History of Force: Exploring the Worldwide Movement Against Habits of Coercion, Bloodshed, and Mayhem. (2004).

REAGAN, RONALD. Annual Convention of the United States League *of Savings Associations*, New Orleans, Louisiana. (16 November 1982).

ROHN, JIM. Goals and Goals Setting. (Jim Rohn International; 2010).

VENEMANA, ANN. UNICEF Representative at Ministerial Press Briefing on World Breastfeeding and Child Health week. (2009).

WOLFE, THOMAS. You Can't Go Home Again. (1940:508).

WOODEN, JOHN. Quoted in One Small Step Can Change Your Life: The Kaizen Way by Robert Maurer. (2004:11).

YEW, LEE KUAN. From Third World to First: The Singapore Story 1965-2000. (2000).

Websites

American Dream. Available at **http://en.wikipedia.org/wiki/American_Dream**

Biography of Lee Kuan Yew. Available at **http://en.wikipedia.org/wiki/Lee_Kuan_Yew.**

Biography of Martin Luther King Jr. Available at **http://en.wikipedia.org/wiki/Martin_Luther_King,_Jr.**

Biography of William H. Foege. Available at **http://en.wikipedia.org/wiki/William_Foege**

Nation-building. Available at **http://en.wikipedia.org/wiki/Nation-building**

Robbins, Anthony. Anthony Robbins Biography. Available at
http://www.anthonyrobbinsfoundation.org/founder/index.php

The Coaching and Mentoring Network "Coach and Mentor Definition" Available at
http://www.coachingnetwork.org.uk/ResourceCentre/WhatAreCoachingAndMe
ntoring.htm

The Salvation Army International Heritage Centre Website "The Biography of
William Booth" Available at

http://www1.salvationarmy.org.uk/

The Salvation Army. Available at
http://en.wikipedia.org/wiki/The_Salvation_Army

About The Author

B obby Udoh is a nation-building evangelist, passionate blogger, impact public speaker, trainer and change agent, who seeks to equip Nigerians with the vision, direction, focus and tools to become nation-builders through speaking engagements, publications, newsletters, conferences and workshops.

Born 4th July 1971 at St Thomas' Hospital, London to Nigerian parents from Eket in Akwa Ibom State. He attended Auntie Margaret International School in Calabar, Federal Government College, Ikot Ekpene and University of Calabar, where he graduated with a BA Honours in History in 1994. In 1996, Bobby relocated to the UK and for 12 years he developed significantly in Sponsorship Sales Management but left to set up, Akwa Holidays, UK, a holiday business. After 3 successful years, he sold the business to focus fully on his passion for nation-building in Nigeria.

Bobby is fully committed to study, practice, teach and inspire nation-building in Nigeria. For weekly nation-building articles, visit: **http://bobbyudoh.com**